Pathways to Public Relations

Student Handbook

Suzanne Lowery Mims
Katherine E. Rowan, Ph.D.
Daniel L. Walsch, Ph.D.

Department of Communication
George Mason University

GEORGE MASON UNIVERSITY | Mason Publishing

Pathways to Public Relations: Student Handbook

Suzanne Lowery Mims, Katherine E. Rowan, Ph.D., Daniel L. Walsch, Ph.D.

ISBN: 978-1-942695-02-8 (Print)

Mason Publishing

The Mason Publishing provides support and resources to the George Mason University community for creating, curating, and disseminating scholarly, creative, and educational works.

Mason Publishing
George Mason University Libraries
4400 University Drive, MS 2FL
Fairfax, VA 22030
www.publishing.gmu.edu

Printed in the United States of America

Introduction: The PR Pathway at George Mason University

The path to a career in any field is a special journey. There is neither one right way nor wrong way to reach your professional goals. Of course, certain jobs require specific training and licensing. Professions like law, medicine, accounting, architecture, and engineering mandate a specific course of advanced study. Some positions also require apprenticeships or other on-the-job experience.

People reach a career in public relations through many different paths. A degree in public relations is not a strict requirement, although many job descriptions will list it as "preferred." To win a job in public relations, however, you will need to demonstrate that you have the knowledge and skills that can be acquired through a college-level public relations curriculum. Employers in public relations seek candidates who:

- Demonstrate competency in professional writing
- Know how to conduct basic client or issue research
- Understand the conventions of journalism, such as attribution, authoritative sources and basics of Associated Press style
- Can synthesize and analyze research and information
- Are familiar with the wide range of materials and digital tools used in PR
- Stay abreast of current events
- Exhibit professional standards of conduct

This handbook has been prepared to help you chart your path and support your studies in public relations. The first section introduces you to the profession, the Mason PR curriculum and the host of ways you can acquire skills and experiences during your years on campus. The next section focuses on skills and provides practical templates and how-to guides to help you complete assignments in your PR courses. The third section walks you through the process of writing a public relations plan, covers basic research, and use of goals, objectives, strategies, and tactics. The last section offers you a primer on working with a client, working in teams, and client communication.

We hope this handbook gives you the motivation and tools to help you take control of your path to public relations. Use this handbook to help develop a plan not just for what courses you will take but for how you will spend your time at Mason.

Finally, we express unbridled excitement at watching your paths unfold. Working in public relations is indeed one of the most creative jobs in the world today. While working in public relations is often very challenging, it is never, ever boring. We can't wait to see where your PR pathway will take you.

Suzanne Lowery Mims   Katherine E. Rowan   Daniel L. Walsch

The Voice of Experience:
Insight Committee Chairman Thomas Hoog

Insight Committee
The Department of Communication

A Message from the Chairman:

Historically, many people have ended up working in public relations by accident rather than by design. Somehow those folks were able to acquire the skills they needed in order to succeed in PR. By choosing the PR concentration for your college studies, you are already well ahead of those who might end up in PR by accident. You are charting a specific path to PR.

You have made a smart decision. Now, I urge you to make the most of your years at Mason. Plan not only what courses you'd like to take but other activities that will contribute to your path to PR. Try working in student media, be the social media director for your club, and consider studying abroad. Plan ahead for the best time and place for an internship. Consider choosing your summer job or part-time job for how it might help build your resume. Wherever you work while in school, pay attention. Just learning how co-workers interact with each other and organization stakeholders is an important lesson.

I believe there are three keys to a successful career in PR. First, you need to develop very strong oral and written communication skills. Second, you have to stay immersed in current events daily and stay connected to news sources. Third, you must maintain professional standards in everything you do. Keep these three things in mind as you continue your studies at Mason and you will be well on your way to a successful career in public relations.

Thomas W. Hoog
Chairman, The Insight Committee, Mason Communication
Vice Chair, Hill and Knowlton Strategies

If I Knew Then, What I Know Now:
Chloe Kingsley-Burt, Class of 2013

 **Alumni Association**

A Message from a Class of 2013 alumna:

It is easy to come to college and think that getting accepted was the last big hurdle. It's OK to revel in your accomplishment, but from the moment you walk onto campus you make choices, big and small, that end up shaping your academic experience, which in turn shapes your professional one. I've heard lots of people say that Communication, and specifically PR, is an easy choice of major. My response is, if it's too easy, you're doing it wrong.

The best way to ensure success after college is to do your best to be successful while you're still here. Have fun and meet people; they become your network. Join clubs and work towards leadership roles; those experiences become your resume. Do lots of different internships; those internships become your work experience. Consider studying abroad or doing research; those things become what differentiate you.

Some of the best advice given that is routinely ignored is to get to know your professors. They are professionals with years of experience, and one of Mason's strengths is that they have all worked, or are continuing to work, in the field. I am not exaggerating when I say that without my professors I would not be where I am now. They sponsored my research, they mentored me through difficult decisions, they introduced me to the right people (who ended up giving me a job!), and they continue to be unwavering supporters and friends. This is not unattainable. I'm not Hermione Granger. I stayed after class one day to say I enjoyed the lesson. I participated in class discussion. A small effort can go a long way.

Working in PR is one of the most fast-paced, exhilarating professions you can have. Prepare for it and get excited. You're well on the way to a successful and rewarding career!

Chloe Kingsley-Burt
Young Alumni Representative,
Alumni Association Board of Directors
Senior Consultant, Booz Allen Hamilton

Contents

Advice from the Real World:
Mason Alumni Share Advice

Listen to the voice of experience: Throughout this book Mason alumni share tips, advice, and thoughts on how to best use your time at Mason in order to create your own path to a successful career in public relations.

Ashley Phillips, Class of 2007
Communications Specialist, ICF International

Write whenever possible, in complete sentences. Even in today's social media driven world where we are forced to fit into a certain number of characters, do not underestimate how far developed writing skills take you in the workplace.

Go to London for the International PR course! It was the best thing I did while at Mason. When else will you have doors to these firms and organizations wide open to you?!

Find a mentor, someone you connect with and look up to in the field, and learn from them. Listen to everything they have to say and chat with them regularly. You will learn a lot more from their past mistakes and stories than you will assuming you have all the answers.

Step outside of the classroom and get involved in organizations and events on campus and in the community that interest you. It's worth the extra effort and time—you know never know who you're going to meet, it could be your next boss!

Section I

The PR Pathway at Mason

Advice from the Real World:
Mason Alumni Share Advice

Claire Dixon, Class of 2014
Marketing Coordinator, Angler Environmental

Honestly, the most useful thing I took away from my PR classes was the ability to quickly form multiple, clear, concise sentences. Although sometimes exhausting, writing and re-writing, and being hit over the head with the AP style guidebook until clutter was minimal, grammar was perfected, and the piece was easy to read, was the most helpful thing I learned. PR helped me become a stronger and more confident writer, something that is essential to what I do as a marketing coordinator. Whether I'm writing a resume, proposal, or tweet, I use the writing skills I learned in my PR classes on a daily basis.

Chapter 1:

Introduction to Public Relations

Advice from the Real World:
Mason Alumni Share Advice

A'Darien Johnson, Class of 2015
IS Sector Communications, Northrop Grumman

I realized my senior year how important PR would impact my career, a little late to say the very least. However, the PR courses I took my last semester of college really helped me transition into the corporate world. I would recommend starting early, exploring as many PR classes as you can, especially the basics like **Intro to PR** (Comm 204/330) to help you understand the discipline and get an idea of what you are getting into. Then, you will be ready  for the writing courses (Comm 391), which are nice during the later part of your college experience because the techniques you will learn will be fresh and in tune for you to take to your internship or first job.

What is Public Relations?

Since World War II, over 500 definitions of "public relations" have been put forth by communication scholars and practitioners. One of the earliest definitions is simply:

the engineering of consent.

From an historical perspective, this short but distinct phrase is significant in that it is the first, formal definition of public relations. Authored by public relations pioneer Edward Bernays, it appeared in, not-so-coincidentally, the first book on public relations: "Crystallizing Public Opinion," published in 1923 by Boni and Liveright. Bernays presented public relations as an act of persuasion. It is, he suggested, an attempt by one entity to motivate another entity or various publics to take certain actions or adapt particular beliefs.

Partnerships, according to this interpretation, are to be formulated to achieve goals that primarily enhance the reputation, level of visibility or "bottom line" of a singular client or organization. It is, of course, fine if others benefit from one entity's strategic efforts, Bernays said. But the key to any act of public relations is for the driver of that act to be in-control of whatever interacting occurs. Other definitions of public relations that followed what Bernays put forth, did not always echo or subscribe to his particular vision. However, many did. Further, public relations as a process by which one entity exerts influence over others continues to dominate how many see this form of communication.

A strategic communication process that builds mutually beneficial relationships between an organization and their publics.

This definition was designed by the Public Relations Society of America in 2012, the organization's first attempt at composing an official, conclusive interpretation of this form of communication in 20 years. It was the result of over 1,400 professionals and scholars being polled as to what they believe should be the definition of public relations (www.prsa.org, 2012). The result highlights such key terms as "mutual," "beneficial," and "relationship."

Collectively, the terms present public relations as an act geared to encourage cooperation and/or collaboration between multiple entities, yet in a manner that is planned, thought-out, and the result of precise discussion, interaction, etc. Additionally and perhaps most significantly, this definition presents public relations not as action initiated by a singular client, but, instead, by multiple entities joining forces to work toward the achievement of a shared goal. Nowhere in this definition is it implied one entity or organization has dominance over another or is, in effect, a "senior partner" over another. Thus, according to the PRSA, public relations can and does represent collaboration between equals—partnership—rather than the attempt by one entity to influence or persuade another.

"Strategic management of competition and conflict for the benefit of one's own organization—and when possible— also for the mutual benefit of the organization and its stakeholders or publics."

Hopefully, this particular definition looks familiar. The most recent of the three showcased here, it can be found in the primary textbook (*Think Public Relations*) of George Mason University's principle public relations course (Wilcox, Cameron, Reber & Shin, 2013). Interestingly, it attempts to touch on the key components of our two previous definitions: persuasion and partnership. On the one hand, the public relations practitioner is portrayed as being an advocate on behalf of his/her client. On the other, the authors recognize the value and importance of multiple organizations benefiting from an act of collaboration. Further, those practicing public relations do not strictly do what they do to satisfy whatever self-interest their client might have.

Also, it is important to note that here public relations is once again showcased as an act of strategic planning. For an effort to communicate to be effective—however one might define that—then it should not be something that is improvised or "winged." At its best, public relations represents steps in a process. These include efforts to identify targeted audiences, formulate reasonable budgets and timelines, develop a sense of any similar efforts that may have been attempted in the past, create specific strategies, including exact communication tools, and identify precise goals by which all steps or actions in the process can be measured or evaluated. According to the authors, any public relations plan in which such steps are not part of the mix are, at best, incomplete. Further, formulating a precise public relations plan is necessary regardless of whether the public relations practitioner seeks to persuade others or simply establish and then maintain partnerships or alliances. Comprehensive plans require such elements as being able to fact-find or conduct research, give great attention to detail, be able to work well with others, and, not surprisingly, communicate in a manner that is understandable and open.

Public Relations Society of America

The Public Relations Society of America is the largest professional organization for professional communicators in the world. There are more than 22,000 PRSA members in 100 regional chapters across the United States. In addition, there are 300 student chapters on college campuses. Established in 1947, the organization has a long history of providing professional development, networking, recognition, and leadership opportunities. PRSA has devised a comprehensive examination to establish professional accreditation. By earning the designation of APR, professionals distinguish themselves as being among the most knowledgeable and accomplished in the field. PRSA also sets standards of excellence and upholds principles of ethics for its members and the profession at large.

To help ensure the profession remains viable, respected and honorable, PRSA's Code of Ethics encourages practitioners to behave ethically and with professional integrity. The PRSA's Code of Ethics emphasizes six core values. This value system offers practitioners a common approach to professional behavior, based on honesty and trust. As a complement to these key values, the Code of Ethics also showcases six "Code Provisions" which commits all public relations professionals to support a free and open society.

Public Relations Society of America
Member Code of Ethics 2000

Public
Relations
Society of
America

Preamble

- ❧ Professional Values
- ❧ Principles of Conduct
- ❧ Commitment and Compliance

This Code applies to PRSA members. The Code is designed to be a useful guide for PRSA members as they carry out their ethical responsibilities. This document is designed to anticipate and accommodate, by precedent, ethical challenges that may arise. The scenarios outlined in the Code provision are actual examples of misconduct. More will be added as experience with the Code occurs.

The Public Relations Society of America (PRSA) is committed to ethical practices. The level of public trust PRSA members seek, as we serve the public good, means we have taken on a special obligation to operate ethically.

The value of member reputation depends upon the ethical conduct of everyone affiliated with the Public Relations Society of America. Each of us sets an example for each other—as well as other professionals—by our pursuit of excellence with powerful standards of performance, professionalism, and ethical conduct.

Emphasis on enforcement of the Code has been eliminated. But, the PRSA Board of Directors retains the right to bar from membership or expel from the Society any individual who has been or is sanctioned by a government agency or convicted in a court of law of an action that is not in compliance with the Code.

Ethical practice is the most important obligation of a PRSA member. We view the Member Code of Ethics as a model for other professions, organizations, and professionals.

PRSA Member Statement of Professional Values

This statement presents the core values of PRSA members and, more broadly, of the public relations profession. These values provide the foundation for the Member Code of Ethics and set the industry standard for the professional practice of public relations.

These values are the fundamental beliefs that guide our behaviors and decisionmaking process. We believe our professional values are vital to the integrity of the profession as a whole.

ADVOCACY

We serve the public interest by acting as responsible advocates for those we represent. We provide a voice in the marketplace of ideas, facts, and viewpoints to aid informed public debate.

HONESTY

We adhere to the highest standards of accuracy and truth in advancing the interests of those we represent and in communicating with the public.

EXPERTISE

We acquire and responsibly use specialized knowledge and experience. We advance the profession through continued professional development, research, and education. We build mutual understanding, credibility, and relationships among a wide array of institutions and audiences.

INDEPENDENCE

We provide objective counsel to those we represent. We are accountable for our actions.

LOYALTY

We are faithful to those we represent, while honoring our obligation to serve the public interest.

FAIRNESS

We deal fairly with clients, employers, competitors, peers, vendors, the media, and the general public. We respect all opinions and support the right of free expression.

PRSA Code Provisions

FREE FLOW OF INFORMATION
Core Principle
Protecting and advancing the free flow of accurate and truthful information is essential to serving the public interest and contributing to informed decisionmaking in a democratic society.

Intent:
To maintain the integrity of relationships with the media, government officials, and the public.

To aid informed decisionmaking.

Guidelines:

A member shall:

- Preserve the integrity of the process of communication.

- Be honest and accurate in all communications.

- Act promptly to correct erroneous communications for which the practitioner is responsible.

- Preserve the free flow of unprejudiced information when giving or receiving gifts by ensuring that gifts are nominal, legal, and infrequent.

Examples of Improper Conduct Under this Provision:

A member representing a ski manufacturer gives a pair of expensive racing skis to a sports magazine columnist, to influence the columnist to write favorable articles about the product.

A member entertains a government official beyond legal limits and/or in violation of government reporting requirements.

COMPETITION

Core Principle

Promoting healthy and fair competition among professionals preserves an ethical climate while fostering a robust business environment.

Intent:

To promote respect and fair competition among public relations professionals. To serve the public interest by providing the widest choice of practitioner options.

Guidelines:

A member shall:

- Follow ethical hiring practices designed to respect free and open competition without deliberately undermining a competitor.

- Preserve intellectual property rights in the marketplace.

Examples of Improper Conduct Under This Provision:

A member employed by a "client organization" shares helpful information with a counseling firm that is competing with others for the organization's business.

A member spreads malicious and unfounded rumors about a competitor in order to alienate the competitor's clients and employees in a ploy to recruit people and business.

DISCLOSURE OF INFORMATION

Core Principle

Open communication fosters informed decisionmaking in a democratic society.

Intent:

To build trust with the public by revealing all information needed for responsible decisionmaking.

Guidelines:
A member shall:

- Be honest and accurate in all communications.
- Act promptly to correct erroneous communications for which the member is responsible.
- Investigate the truthfulness and accuracy of information released on behalf of those represented.
- Reveal the sponsors for causes and interests represented.
- Disclose financial interest (such as stock ownership) in a client's organization. Avoid deceptive practices.

Examples of Improper Conduct Under this Provision:
Front groups: A member implements "grass roots" campaigns or letter-writing campaigns to legislators on behalf of undisclosed interest groups.

Lying by omission: A practitioner for a corporation knowingly fails to release financial information, giving a misleading impression of the corporation's performance.

A member discovers inaccurate information disseminated via a website or media kit and does not correct the information.

A member deceives the public by employing people to pose as volunteers to speak at public hearings and participate in "grass roots" campaigns.

SAFEGUARDING CONFIDENCES

Core Principle
Client trust requires appropriate protection of confidential and private information.

Intent:
To protect the privacy rights of clients, organizations, and individuals by safeguarding confidential information.

Guidelines:
A member shall:

- Safeguard the confidences and privacy rights of present, former, and prospective clients and employees.
- Protect privileged, confidential, or insider information gained from a client or organization.
- Immediately advise an appropriate authority if a member discovers that confidential information is being divulged by an employee of a client company or organization.

Examples of Improper Conduct Under This Provision:
A member changes jobs, takes confidential information, and uses that information in the new position to the detriment of the former employer.

A member intentionally leaks proprietary information to the detriment of some other party.

CONFLICTS OF INTEREST

Core Principle
Avoiding real, potential or perceived conflicts of interest builds the trust of clients, employers, and the public.

Intent:
To earn trust and mutual respect with clients or employers.

To build trust with the public by avoiding or ending situations that put one's personal or professional interests in conflict with society's interests.

Guidelines:
A member shall:

- Act in the best interests of the client or employer, even subordinating the member's personal interests.

- Avoid actions and circumstances that may appear to compromise good business judgment or create a conflict between personal and professional interests.

- Disclose promptly any existing or potential conflict of interest to affected clients or organizations.

- Encourage clients and customers to determine if a conflict exists after notifying all affected parties.

Examples of Improper Conduct Under This Provision:
The member fails to disclose that he or she has a strong financial interest in a client's chief competitor.

The member represents a "competitor company" or a "conflicting interest" without informing a prospective client.

ENHANCING THE PROFESSION

Core Principle
Public relations professionals work constantly to strengthen the public's trust in the profession.

Intent:
To build respect and credibility with the public for the profession of public relations. To improve, adapt, and expand professional practices.

Guidelines:
A member shall:

- Acknowledge that there is an obligation to protect and enhance the profession.

- Keep informed and educated about practices in the profession to ensure ethical conduct.
- Actively pursue personal professional development.
- Decline representation of clients or organizations that urge or require actions contrary to this Code.
- Accurately define what public relations activities can accomplish.
- Counsel subordinates in proper ethical decisionmaking.
- Require that subordinates adhere to the ethical requirements of the Code.
- Report practices not in compliance with the Code, whether committed by PRSA members or not, to the appropriate authority.

Examples of Improper Conduct Under This Provision:
A PRSA member declares publicly that a product the client sells is safe, without disclosing evidence to the contrary.

A member initially assigns some questionable client work to a non-member practitioner to avoid the ethical obligation of PRSA membership.

PRSA Member Code of Ethics Pledge

I pledge:

To conduct myself professionally, with truth, accuracy, fairness, and responsibility to the public; To improve my individual competence and advance the knowledge and proficiency of the profession through continuing research and education; And to adhere to the articles of the Member Code of Ethics 2000 for the practice of public relations as adopted by the governing Assembly of the Public Relations Society of America.

I understand and accept that there is a consequence for misconduct, up to and including membership revocation.

And, I understand that those who have been or are sanctioned by a government agency or convicted in a court of law of an action that is not in compliance with the Code may be barred from membership or expelled from the Society.

Signature

Date

PRSA's Silver Anvil Case Histories

For each of the past nearly 60 years, the Public Relations Society of America has been honoring what it judges to be the best in public relations practices. The result is the recognition of a multitude of individuals and organizations to promote clients, enhance the reputation of the profession, and display a high level of unmatched professional skill. Among the specific categories under which practitioners are judged and ultimately honored are: public service, marketing, community relations, integrated communication, events and observances, brand management, internal communication, multicultural communication, crisis communication, global communication, investor relations, issue management, and public affairs.

To learn more about these awards and the specific honorees, students are urged to visit **www.prsa.org/awards/search**. Here are detailed explanations of the many Silver Anvil recipients, a breakdown of the steps taken in their specific campaigns, and background information on what influenced the array of public relations professionals to create the various strategies they did to achieve successful results. Collectively, this information provides students with a thorough glimpse of the many details that comprise effective public relations, regardless if the purpose is to promote, persuade or establish lasting partnerships. Such data can also serve as an inspiration to communication students who are seriously considering careers in public relations. By viewing detailed descriptions of what has been judged to be the "best of the best" in public relations over the past half-century, today's students and tomorrow leading professional communicators can gain greater appreciation of the value of the positive impact public relations can and does play in society.

Chapter 2:

Mason's PR Curriculum & Opportunities

Advice from the Real World:
Mason Alumni Share Advice

Lisa Buzzelli, Class of 2010
Communications Specialist, Ikun, LLC

Many students often overlook the fact that Mason
has so many resources available to those who are
on the job hunt. By utilizing Career Services, I was
able to have a competitive resume, and prepare
for what's next through several workshops. My
advice? Start early, be persistent, and don't overlook the small achievements. We have many tal-
ented alumni, so connect with them and ask questions.

A Guide to Required and Elective PR Classes

To give you a solid foundation, four classes are required of all communication majors (the core) and another four are required for public relations concentrators. Then there are electives for PR concentrators. You choose 9 to 15 credit hours from among the electives. Some students use their electives to build their expertise in writing, videography, or social media in public relations. Others enroll in public relations study abroad. Still others use the electives to take honors research classes or hands-on, one-credit classes and three-credit internships.

Talk to your adviser, faculty, fellow students, local professionals, family, and friends to guide your journey through the communication major and public relations concentration. Visit the communication department website: **http://communication.gmu. edu/programs/la-ba-com**. Locate the advising section of the website to schedule an appointment: **https://communication.acuityscheduling.com/schedule.php**.

You will find that good times for appointments begin after the last day to add a class and before registration for the upcoming semester. For example, mid-September through mid-October is usually a good time to schedule advising for spring classes.

The communication major requires 39 credit hours, not including **Communication 100: Public Speaking** or **Communication 101: Interpersonal Communication**. Here is an overview of the communication major with a public relations concentration.

Required Communication Core (12 credits)

200 Communication Theory introduces you to the major. You learn theories to help you think about why people act and communicate as they do. This information helps you to be a strategic communicator; that is, someone who can think of several evidence-based options for achieving a communication goal, such as promoting a healthful practice or considering a different point of view. You need to receive at a C or better in this class before taking communication classes at the 300-level.

300 Foundations of Public Communication is the writing intensive class in the major. In this class, you research and write analyses, ones that you may want to submit to an academic conference for presentation. For example, you will learn how to analyze the persuasive effects of a speech, a cultural artifact such as a popular song, or a campaign, such as efforts to gain human rights or protect animals. This class focuses on humanistic forms of research.

305 Foundations of Intercultural Communication explores the ways in which culture shapes identities. Knowledge of intercultural communication assists public relations professionals in listening to and respecting many stakeholders such as men, women, members of differing ethnic groups, and differing regions of the world. In a global economy, those who can communicate with people from many cultures are essential employees.

400 Research Methods delves into steps for conducting social science research. In public relations, we often use surveys, focus groups, and analyses of social and traditional media to learn about our stakeholders and to encourage them to consider a new product or practice. This class assists you in conducting research and in determining whether a study or survey has been well done.

490 Honors Research Methods is the equivalent course to COMM 400, but it is taught at the honors level. Like 400, it delves into steps for conducting social science research. In public relations, we often use surveys, focus groups, and analyses of social and traditional media to learn about stakeholders and encourage them to consider a new product or think about stigmatized groups in a fresh way. This class is a two-semester sequence. You create a research module during the first semester (COMM 490) and during the spring semester you take COMM 491 where you conduct research and present findings at a CHSS-wide conference at Mason. By taking this sequence, you earn the prestigious Honor in Communication designation on your transcript and diploma.

Required Courses for PR Concentrators (12 credits)

Advice from alumni and faculty: Graduates of our program recommend that you do NOT take all your public relations classes in one semester. They also tell us that you should NOT wait until your last semester to take all classes required of PR concentrators. These classes help you build skills and values. You will learn more if you give yourself time to absorb one set of skills and then build upon those with others.

204 Introduction to Public Relations is the first public relations class you should take in the concentration. It teaches you what public relations is and gives you a sense of public relations as it is practiced by corporate, government, and nonprofit groups. Most importantly, you learn the ethical principles that should guide all public relations professionals.

303 Writing Across the Media is skills class you should take soon after Communication 200. The class meets in classrooms filled with computers. You research and write news and feature articles for the mass media. You also learn to pitch stories and contact sources for statements.

331 Advanced Principles in Public Relations is an upper-level class. In it, you put all that you have learned previously toward assisting clients for an entire semester. Unlike in other classes, you meet your clients early in the semester and conduct research to think with them about the sorts of interventions that would assist them. Then you draw from your analysis of the client's goal and stakeholders' concerns to build and implement a public relations plan for the client, one that meets your, the client's, and the stakeholders' needs and standards.

430 Persuasion is a senior-level course on research and theories concerning attitude and behavior change. Public relations professionals often help clients who want to be better known, have their products purchased, or have their services used. Bringing about attitudinal and behavioral change is tough. This class gives you a set of evidence-backed approaches.

Electives for Public Relations Concentrators (choose 9 credit hours)

Ideally, students should take these classes after taking COMM 204 Introduction to Public Relations and COMM 303 Writing across the Media. The best way to guide your elective choices is to learn what faculty members and advisers recommend as well as what alumni and fellow students suggest. Here is a list of the electives you can take as a public relations concentrator. We offer detailed descriptions of classes that are frequently recommended. You can find descriptions of all classes in the Mason online catalogue.

202 Media and Society

230 Case Studies in Persuasion

260 Basic Debate Theory and Practice

261 Theories of Argumentation

302 Foundations of Mass Communication

320 Business and Professional Communication

335 Organizational Communication

351 News Writing and Reporting. In this class, you learn to research and write hard news, particularly news about current events. Developing reporting skill gives you a sense of what journalists look for when evaluating news. Deepening your knowledge of news reporting makes you especially effective in public relations.

359 Media Management

362 Argument and Public Policy

375 Mass Communication Advertising and Promotion. This is THE class for learning about advertising. It covers audience needs, channel selection, message design as well as advertising history, regulation, media buying, and campaigns.

388 Special Topics in Public Relations. There is at least one special topics in public relations class offered each semester. Take a look at the offerings numbered COMM 388, especially as you enter your junior and senior years. These classes focus on distinctive skills and topics, such as social media; science, media, and outreach, and crisis communication.

389 Public Relations for Associations and Nonprofits. Would you like to work for the American Automobile Association in Fairfax or Human Rights Watch in Washington, D.C.? How about the Society of Interventional Radiology also located in Fairfax? The Washington metropolitan area is home to thousands of professional and trade associations. This class provides an ideal context for learning about them. In this class, you become familiar with many of these organizations. You will be encouraged to visit at least one, and you will produce a public relations plan to address an issue of concern for an association or nonprofit.

390 Issues in Public Relations. The heart of public relations involves deep understanding of audiences. In this class, you explore contemporary issues confronting public relations professionals. Perhaps you will explore ethics and corporate responsibility. You might analyze a contemporary hot issue such as genetically modified food and whether it should be labeled as such. Or you might analyze the challenges of a client accused of stealing trade secrets. Typically, you explore the perspectives of several groups on some challenging concern, learn options for assisting clients who face a tough issue, and develop strategic plans for helping your client while still remaining true to your carefully considered ethical stance.

391 Writing for Public Relations. This writing-intensive class is an ideal way to build your portfolio and skills. Instructors use a first-version, final-version system, where you do your best work, get feedback, revise, and then receive a grade on your final version. This system helps you learn and improves the quality of your writing samples. The class covers hard and feature news releases, profiles, fact sheets, backgrounders, proposals, public service announcements, social media, and graphic design.

392 Public Relations Study Abroad. This class is one many students say is their favorite. Currently, there is a public relations in London study abroad class, one in Milan, Italy, and another in Munich, Germany. Each involves learning about public relations and culture in the respective city. Talk to your adviser and fellow students about these options. Be alert for sign up deadlines.

411 Public Relations Practicum

433 Environmental Communication. We are proud to offer environmental communication. In this class, you learn about some of the great environmental communication campaigns and best practices for engaging with the public about fundamental issues such as clean water, flooding, toxic waste, and climate change. You also learn steps for engaging stakeholders on these issues without making them feel fatalistic.

440 Ceremonial Speech Writing and Performance

450 Communication Internship. PR faculty and alumni of our program recommend that you experience at least two internships by taking COMM 450: Internship in Communication, a three-credit class, *twice*. Why? Most public relations professionals get their jobs by doing several internships. Another good reason to intern while you are in school is that many internship supervisors *require that you be enrolled in college to be considered for an internship experience*. See the communication department website for internship requirements and a list of employers eager for interns. Learn more at **http:// communication.gmu.edu/undergraduate/internships-careers**.

454 Free Speech and Ethics. This class is an essential one for those planning to practice public relations in the United States, as well as for any U. S. citizen. It covers the establishment of free speech and a free press in the Bill of Rights, a part of the U.S. Constitution, and the implications of free speech for public life, public relations as a profession, and journalism. The class teaches students the legal basis for determining when libel has occurred. A core focus of this class is also ethics on important matters such as use of copyrighted materials and truthfulness in communicating with clients and stakeholders. This course is often used to meet the university's "synthesis" requirement, in addition to counting as a public relations concentration elective.

Additional Courses in Communication (6 credits)

To complete the major, take an additional 6 credits. You can choose any communication courses for this purpose. Most choose from among the public relations electives listed above, the one-credit classes listed below, study abroad, internships, and honors classes. Select courses at the 300- or 400-level because you must have 45 credits at 300- or 400-level to graduate.

One-Credit Courses Limited to 10 Credits (many are hands-on, project classes, good for skill and portfolio building). Of the 39 credits applied to the major, no more than 10 credits may be in these courses:

140 Forensics Seminar in Creative Arts

141 Forensics Seminar in Recreative Arts

142 Forensics Seminar in Debate: Affirmative Strategies

143 Forensics Seminar in Debate: Negative Strategies

145 Newspaper Workshop 1

148 Radio Workshop I

157 Video Workshop

340 Forensics Seminar in Creative Arts

341 Forensics Seminar in Recreative Arts

342 Forensics Seminar in Debate: Affirmative Strategies

343 Forensics Seminar in Debate: Negative Strategies

345 Newspaper Workshop II. Students in this hands-on class research and write news stories for Mason's student newspaper, *The Fourth Estate*. This experience is invaluable for all those seeking careers in public relations or journalism. You come away with published stories and knowledge of what counts as news.

346 Yearbook Workshop

348 Radio Workshop II

398 Research Practicum in Communication

450 Internship in Communication

451 Facilitating Communication Education

452 Media Production Practicum. Students who have built their videography skills should consider a class focused on a media production project. Contact the course instructor for specifics.

491 Honors Research Project in Communication. Top students find that they enjoy research. Alumni tell us that research skills are valued by employers. Take advantage of opportunities to work closely with faculty on a question that interests you. This kind of class frequently concludes with opportunities to present your work at an on-campus academic conference.

498 Research Projects in Communication. This class is an additional one where students can conduct full-scale research projects in consultation with a faculty member. A typical project: Let's say you wonder what messages would most encourage people to value a threatened species native to Virginia. If you have a question like that, in this class, you and a faculty member might develop, conduct, and analyze an online survey to learn which messages were most effective with key stakeholders.

499 Independent Study in Communication

Career Specific Organizations and Activities

Mason offers many opportunities for students to learn about public relations and gain hands-on experience. The student chapter of such national professional organizations like PRSA and SPJ link students to a wide network of working professionals and to a vast supply of resources. These connections are designed to help students gain greater insight into the industry.

Campus organizations also offer students the chance to take on leadership positions. As an executive or board member, participants will have the opportunity to create and participate in programs as well as gain experiences that help to demonstrate employers and internships that you have some working knowledge of PR.

PRSSA: THE STUDENT CHAPTER

Public Relations Society of America

Faculty Advisor: Professor Sergei Samoilenko

The Public Relations Student Society of America (PRSSA) is the foremost organization for students interested in public relations and communications. We seek to advance the public relations profession by nurturing generations of future professionals. We advocate rigorous academic standards for public relations education, the highest ethical principles and diversity in the profession.

Who We Are

PRSSA (**http://gmuprssa.onmason.com/**) is made up of more than 11,000 students and advisers organized into 300 plus chapters in the United States and one in Argentina. We are headquartered in New York City, and led by a National Committee of PRSSA and PRSA members. We have a rich history of support from our parent organization, the Public Relations Society of America (PRSA), which offers professional development, networking opportunities and news.

PRSSA helps you enhance your education, broaden your network and launch your career in public relations.

Membership Benefits

Enhance Your Education. We can recommend great places to study public relations, and then help you get the experience,

Mason PRSSA Members at the Thoth Awards

achievements and practical knowledge employers are seeking. PRSSA offers internship listings, competitions, and Chapter and National leadership opportunities; scholarships and leadership awards; and publications, news and social media to keep you updated on industry trends.

Broaden Your Network. PRSSA can connect you to lifelong opportunity, experience, and professional growth. Develop valuable relationships with future colleagues through PRSSA National and regional events, PRSSA Chapters, PRSSA social media or Chapter and National leadership opportunities. Meet current professionals at your PRSA sponsor Chapter, through the Champions for PRSSA or by searching the PRSA member directory.

Launch Your Career. As a PRSSA member, you can use the PRSA Job center to find public relations employment opportunities all over the world. You also may join PRSA for just $60 a year as an Associate Member when you graduate, connecting you to 110 Chapters, 16 Professional Interest Sections, and resources especially for new professionals.

Join the Mason chapter of PRSSA now to start getting ahead.

THE CAMPUS CHAPTER

Society of Professional Journalists

Faculty advisor: Professor Beth Jannery

The Society of Professional Journalists (SPJ)—https://www.spj.org/— is an organization on campus for young, aspiring journalists to meet, learn, and grow together through professional networking and the help of their peers.

The Mason chapter of SPJ is largely run by students and guided by a faculty advisor. It is an excellent organization for anyone with an interest or passion for journalism and writing, and members are not required to have a major or minor in journalism. This is also a good organization to join if you are looking to get involved and hold a leadership position on campus. Most significantly, the highest benefit of joining is the many networking opportunities. For example, even though SPJ at Mason is young, the D.C. chapter is well established and works with us so we may attend conferences and events with numerous established journalist professionals in attendance. By going to such conferences, you as a member will be able to learn a lot, all while gaining potential work contacts.

Mission Statement

As a professional society, we pride ourselves in upholding a high standard of journalism and the first amendment, and in striving to create a place where those with a passion can grow and thrive among those who share that passion with them.

Several other campus organizations can provide you with hands-on experience in event management, publicity, media relations, social media relations, product promotion, and writing for public relations. Contact the **Office of Student Involvement—http://si.gmu.edu/registered-student-organizations/**—to review opportunities to get involved in student organizations. Contact the **Office of Student Media—http://studentmedia.gmu.edu/index.html**—for opportunities with Mason's online newspaper, cable station, and radio station, as well as student-run publications.

Fourth Estate is George Mason University's official student-run news outlet: (**http://gmufourthestate.com/**).

Mason Cable Network is the student operated television network airing 24/7 on channel 61.1 to approximately 6,000 residents on the Fairfax Campus. MCN produces and broadcast news, sports, and entertainment videos, and airs submissions by students: **http://masoncablenetwork.com/**.

WGMU Radio is the pulse of Mason, the station for students and by students. WGMU broadcasts a wide array of music, talk, sports, and news programming. WGMU is the flagship station for George Mason's Men's and Women's Basketball team, part of the Go Mason Digital Network: **http://wgmuradio.com/**.

The Insight Committee

The Insight Committee of the George Mason University's Department of Communication was formed to build and enhance relationships between the department, the students, and the larger community of practicing public relations and communication professionals. The committee also strives to maintain an ongoing dialogue to help focus the department's research and instruction on meeting the current demands of the professional communication community.

The Insight Committee is chaired presently by Thomas Hoog, vice chair of Hill & Knowlton Strategies, where he has served in a number of leadership roles, including as its U.S. president. The committee is comprised of senior working professionals from various paths of communication including corporations, associations, law and public affairs, PR agencies and consulting, government, and nonprofits. The committee meets regularly to provide guidance and to develop specific programs for the student population.

Annual Communication Forum

The Insight Committee annually sponsors an event during the fall semester to bring students and working communication professionals together for a unique experience. The event generally features a keynote speaker and a panel of experts to discuss a current aspect of professional communication. Students then participate in a Q & A session with invited guests in a process somewhat similar to speed dating: students stay seated at tables for 10-12 and the experts rotate among them every 15 minutes. Recent forums have featured:

- Content Marketing and the Art of Storytelling (2015) Keynote speaker Kathryn McCarthy, CEO, ThinkGeek & GeekNet

- #AllThingsSocial (2014) Keynote speaker Aaron Sherinian, the United Nations Foundation

- Taming the Communication Beast (2013) Keynote speaker Chuck Todd, NBC-TV chief political correspondent and host, Meet the Press

#AllThingsSocial Keynote speaker Aaron Sherinian, United Nations Foundation

- Business and Professional Communication: A view from the street. Keynote speaker: Anthony Williams, former mayor, Washington, D.C.

- Communication Career Forum (2012) Keynote speaker Jim Clifton, CEO, Gallup

- The AIDS Quilt (2011) Presentation of 104 quilt panels throughout the student union

- Newspapers in the Digital Age (2010) with speakers from The Washington Post, local newspapers and media scholars

Guest panelists include experts in corporate, government, and nonprofit communication. Among the panelists in recent years are:

- Bill Aydelott, Director-Producer-Cameraman, Waverly Motion Pictures

- Lindsey Spindle, Share Our Strength, No Kid Hungry

- Gary Goldhammer, Storyteller and Chief Digital Strategist, Group SJR

- Angie Goff, NBC-WRC-TV 4 anchor

- Linda Smith, Digital Marketing Strategist, Sage Commnications

- Jill Moss, USAID

- Andrew Bleeker, H&K Strategies

- Lauren Green, Northrop Grumman

- Mike McCurry, former White House press secretary

- Anne Gearan, diplomatic correspondent, the Washington Post

- Maureen Knightly, director of communications, U.S. Peace Corps

- Scott Murphy, mcgarrybowen advertising agency

Study Abroad Programs

"Study abroad. It is one of the best things you can do to prepare to work in our global world." At George Mason's 2011 annual communication department symposium, this was the message of keynote speaker Jim Clifton, chairman and CEO of Gallup, one of the world's leading public opinion research firms. Employers, he said, recognize that an international study experience helps students appreciate the interconnected nature of business and communication across the globe today.

In keeping with the vision articulated by Clifton, Mason Study Abroad offers a variety of programs throughout the academic year and during winter, spring, and summer breaks. In addition, the center coordinates internships in locations around the world. PR students have enjoyed the opportunity to study international public relations through the winter program in London.

International Public Relations Study Abroad Program in London

The dynamic field of public relations has reached a global level, crossing social, cultural, and political borders. In this winter break program, students are granted direct access to world leaders in PR agencies, news media, corporate communication, public affairs, and public information.

In this two-week, fast track program, students will hear from senior management executives on how they meet the challenges of global PR in today's social mediated, participatory environment. Site visits in recent years have included several of the world's leading public relations agencies like H+K Strategies, Edelman, Ketchum and Bell Pottinger; the British Broadcasting Corporation; the U.S. Embassy; the London Telegraph; an international corporate communication department; and an international nonprofit association.

Students will examine a wide range of current public relations issues and learn how agencies and in-house PR professionals manage and respond to them. Through this course, students will:

- ❧ Obtain a better understanding of the challenges and capabilities of today's international public relations.

PR Study Abroad Students in London
with Professor Suzanne Mims

- Understand and apply communication theories and ethical principles in international public relations efforts.

- Study the impact of technology on public relations practices and the convergence of PR, advertising, and marketing into integrated digital communication.

- Understand the pressure placed on PR today by the demand for original content, mobile communication, corporate social responsibility, and sustainability.

- Learn how PR agencies and in-house PR departments function and the nature of the agency-client relationship, from both the agency and client perspective.

- Hear from entry-level to senior management executives how to chart a career in public relations.

Students stay in a hotel in downtown London and have the opportunity to explore various parts of this historic city in their spare time. The program usually includes several additional special events, like a day trip to Oxford or Canterbury, a citywide bus tour, a theater performance and pub dining.

PR Study Abroad Students at *London Telegraph*

Advice from the Real World:
Mason Alumni Share Advice

Fred McGrath, Class of 2013
Policy Center Assistant, American Conservative Union

Despite graduating with honors communication and economics degrees, the fact that I did not have much previous relevant work experience really made it rather tough for me to land a job. While it may be difficult and time consuming, try to work a part time internship while you are taking classes. While that paid on-campus or retail job may look appealing, employers like to see that you have actually had some hands on time in the corporate world. I would highly recommend trying to seek  out an internship with a larger, reputable company, even if it is unpaid. This will pay dividends down the road for you, as employers will take you much more seriously.

As far as courses go, I think that the more writing based ones you can take, the better. This is a skill that few have, and is valued rather highly by employers. Also, consider trying to complement your degree with a minor in a field such as business or economics.

Chapter 3:

Charting Your Path

Advice from the Real World:
Mason Alumni Share Advice

Keli Harris, Class of 2013
Marketing Associate, Transportation General, Inc.

No one tells you about the struggles of trying to prove yourself to an employer despite the education you've earned. In my Writing for PR course, I built a portfolio of writing samples to showcase skills when looking for a job. This was the single most important thing I took with me when I left Mason because it has impressed every single person I've ever interviewed with! If I had to do it all over again, I would have participated in internships for the experience. Employers want the perfect combination, education plus experience. Everything you do in your courses has a purpose after college, just be patient and give it everything you have! Remember that you are the preparer of your future.

Gaining Practical Experience:
Courses, Jobs and Internships

How can I get started working in public relations without having any experience? Graduating seniors often get discouraged when reading "experience preferred or required" in job postings. With smart planning, however, you can acquire hands-on experience in public relations during your college years through your courses, extra-curricular activities, part-time work, and internships. The key is to make gaining practical experience an integral part of your college studies.

Course work: Your public relations courses include assignments that employers will view as practical experience. Students routinely include PR plans, projects, and portfolios on resumes and LinkedIn profiles (see sample resumes). Make sure any assignment you present as a work sample is rigorously edited and error free.

> *"(At my interview)...they were impressed with the PR projects I had listed on my resume from your Principles of Public Relations class... I brought hard copies of my PR plan from Coach My Clip project...What impressed them was that these were not just class assignments, but projects executed for actual clients." Mariam Aburdineh, Class of 2013*

Campus activities, volunteer and paid jobs: Are you the social media manager for your sorority? Working part-time as an RA? Helping to promote a major campus event? Writing for a fashion blog or Fourth Estate? In choosing how you spend your free time or what part-time job to seek, consider if and how the experience will contribute to your hands-on learning about public relations. Remember: PR is a strategic communication process that helps build and maintain relationships between an organization and their publics. Think about how some of your activities might contribute to your relationship-building experience.

Internship in Communication COMM 450: Through this course, you will earn three credits and complete an internship designed to give you the practical experience of working in public relations for a supervisor in an organization. Plan to take this course in your junior or senior year. An added benefit of the course is that you will develop a plan for the most important client you'll ever have: you. In this assignment, students map out a plan for seeking and preparing for their post-graduate employment. In recent years, students in this course have completed internships for the following:

- ABC
- AOL
- BBC
- CBS
- Radio
- Clear Channel Broadcasting
- Fairfax Government
- Northrop Grumman
- Celebrate Fairfax (PR)
- Wolftrap
- NAB

- National Science Foundation
- NBC Today
- U.S. Speaker of the House
- White House
- American Society of Engineers
- USO
- USA Today
- VW Group of America
- Voice of America
- Washington Redskins

Internship: In addition to COMM 450, many students apply for and arrange an internship that fits with their course schedules, commute, and part-time jobs. Students intern with local PR firms, federal, state and local government, corporations, small businesses, non-profit, and associations. While some internships are paid, most are not. The key to finding and landing an internship is to conduct a thorough search, network with family and friends for opportunities, apply before the deadline, and submit a professional application with solid references. Students sometimes wonder why one student won an internship but others not? The answer is often: because he or she applied. See the "Guide to Internships" section.

A Guide to Internships

A quick Google search will give you thousands of results to pursue but you should begin with whom you know and what you are most interested in. Network with family and friends for possible leads. Search for local organizations that match your interests, such as fashion, sports, health or entertainment. It seems a daunting task at first but becomes more manageable (and exciting) once you zero in on realistic options.

Here are just a few of the sites offering help in finding an internship:

PRSSA Internship Center: One of the many reasons why you should join the campus chapter of the Public Relations Society of America. On this site, you can upload your resume for potential employers to view and search through the PRSA internship listing (**http://prssa.prsa.org/career/internships/**).

Internships.com, a Chegg service: This site offers a wealth of information on how to find an internship in public relations, how to prepare for the interview, how to write a resume and more. You can even search by terms like, "public relations intern" and "Washington, D.C." Try it! (**http://www.internships.com/public-relations**)

Looksharp also offers resources for finding internships and jobs in public relations along with company profiles (**https://www.looksharp.com/**).

LinkedIn also offers students a way to connect with possible internships in public relations (**https://www.linkedin.com/job/pr-intern-jobs/**).

For example, this internship opening was posted on LinkedIn in 2015:

Intern - PR
Practice Area: Public Affairs

Responsibilities: The Intern is responsible for assisting with implementing and monitoring projects within a specific set of accounts under the direction of the supervisor. S/he works closely with and supports the needs of the account teams. Responsibilities include, but are not limited to:

- Basic understanding of principles of PR
- Basic understanding of clients' business
- Participation in brainstorms when invited by the supervisor
- Read and identify media clips from clipping services and on-line resources
- Assist with monitoring client competition coverage
- Pitch the media under the direction of the supervisor

- Assist with preparation of press kits for distribution
- Update media lists
- Assist with compilation of media coverage reports
- Familiarity with AP style
- Draft pitch letters and/or email pitch memos to vendors with the approval of the supervisor
- Conduct and compile research
- Basic understanding of key client information, including general business strategy, industry issues, products and services, key customers, and competitors in the marketplace
- Basic understanding of research and media list building tools (Factiva, Edge, etc.)

The intern must be able to work effectively with a variety of account service staff within a specific set of accounts. S/he must have good organizational skills and the ability to adapt to new conditions, assignments, and deadlines. S/he must have solid knowledge of MS Office Suite and superior verbal and written communication skills. The Intern is generally someone who has recently graduated with a Bachelor's degree and is looking for entry-level experience in Public Relations. S/he must demonstrate the ability to become a strong writer. Familiarity with the Public Relations discipline through past coursework or other internships is desirable. Basic Qualifications: Intern candidates must have interest in the public relations field and possess good interpersonal and communication skills with the ability to work effectively with others.

Tips for Intern Success

Article reprinted courtesy of Internships.com

Using your free time wisely during your summer breaks from college is extremely important. On a small scale, free time during the summer may mean going to the beach or checking your Facebook page. But on a large scale, three summer months can be a great opportunity for picking up skills that give you an edge over other college students.

Pursuing a lifeguard certification or waiting tables at restaurants are typical college student job options. While both jobs sound fun, the value of using your time that way is short-lived. And, it can be harder for you when it comes time to graduate to demonstrate on your resume how this work sets you apart from other candidates. Avoid this scenario by using your summer months to benefit your career in the long-term. These 7 tips can help you find great summer internships for college students:

- **Choose the field:** Summer internships for students are your chance to explore career options with low commitment. You aren't expected to make a lifelong career decision. But choose smartly—the field might help you get a leg up when it's time to find a real job. A great tool to help you decide the best fit is the internships.com *Internship Predictor*. Use this tool to get some practical ideas to guide your search for summer internships for college students.

- **Choose the location:** Enjoy considering possible locations for your summer internship, but be realistic. Think about housing, transportation, and proximity to family and friends. You can use the Company Directory on Internships.com, search for summer internships by category or college major or search for internships based on location.

- **Have your resume ready:** To find a summer internship program, college students, even high school students, should be prepared with an organized, error-free record of your education and work experience. Get a head start by building your Profile - a fast way to the professional resume you need for applications and interviews. Summer internship programs offer exposure to the real-world demands of applying for, landing, and keeping a job. Getting your resume right is a good first step.

- **Get ready for the interview:** If you are going to meet your future employer, you need to look the part. Trim your hair and wear neat and appropriate attire. If it's a phone interview, be prepared and polite. In both scenarios, do some prep work— be prepared to explain and discuss everything you included on your resume, think about how the college courses you've taken so far have prepared you for this job, have a few questions about the job and company ready to ask (they will ask you if you have any questions), and review your qualifications, strengths, and weaknesses so you are ready to provide good answers. Taking the Intern Certification Program can help you learn more about what employers will expect of you and prepare you for a good discussion.

- **Create a realistic budget:** Summer internships for undergraduates, while valuable learning experiences, often are unpaid positions. Consider the money you will need during the summer and when it comes time to buy books for the fall semester back at college. Work up a budget so you know what you can realistically handle in the money department. Sticking to your internship program schedule and a budget can help you make the most of your summer away from college.

- **Get your papers organized:** When you apply for a summer internship you may need some documents beyond your resume. College transcripts and letters of recommendation are great pieces of information to share with your potential employer when your job experience is limited. And be sure to bring your identification.

- **Search for an internship on internships.com:** This is a no-brainer. Go to internships.com to find the summer internship for you (**http://www. internships.com/search/guided**). It's a comprehensive listing that has the info you need to find the summer program for you.

Internships.com Sample Description Public Relations Intern

(See: **http://www.internships.com/employer/resources/internships/public_relations**)

Description

Company, a small public relations firm handling busy clients, is looking for an intern interested in learning all aspects of the public relations field. The intern who fills this position should expect to learn the field from top to bottom, and will graduate from this program ready to enter any fast-paced public relations firm with excellent skills. It's essential that applicants to this position have excellent communication skills, demonstrate creativity, and understand the importance of attending to even the smallest details.

Responsibilities

- Monitor all forms of media
- Schedule and coordinate speaking engagements, appearances, photo shoots, and other special events
- Write press releases and other materials
- Screen phone calls
- Assist with mailings, print production
- Create interview preparation materials
- Compile contact lists
- Search for press clippings
- Create or update databases
- Greet guests and clients

Requirements

Students applying for this internship must have strong communication skills and should be majoring in Public Relations, Communications, Marketing or Journalism. Applicants should also have strong writing skills, as well as a solid understanding of social media. Only interns proficient with Microsoft Excel and other Microsoft Office applications should apply.

Majors

Public Relations, Marketing, Communications, Journalism

Building a Portfolio of Work

Students often find themselves in a panic when an internship or job application asks for a writing sample. What should I use? Do I really have any "PR samples?"

Your Mason communication courses offer many assignments that will help you demonstrate your strategic, analytic, and writing skills. Each of the public relations courses requires you to complete one if not many written works that will qualify as a "PR writing sample." Students in **Writing for PR** (COMM 391) produce a series of written and digital pieces and usually create a coherent portfolio of work.

A word of caution: any sample that earned less than an A may do you more harm than good. . . unless you correct that draft for the errors or suggested revisions.

What work qualifies as a writing sample:

- News release
- Digital release or media advisory
- Profile, brief biography
- Media pitch email
- Feature article or release
- Published news article (IV Estate, university websites, other media)
- Blog posts
- PSA
- Client correspondence, planning memo
- Backgrounder
- Fact Sheet
- Brochure
- Media kit
- About Us or other website pages
- Infographic (representing data, timeline, facts)
- Twitter campaign (strategic, objective-driven)
- Facebook campaign (strategic, objective-driven)
- Case history or "PR snapshot"
- Exemplar campaign analysis
- Slide presentation of PR-related issue, news, campaign

- Public relations plan, outline or proposal for client
- Public relations plan for in-class exercise
- Social media engagement plan or campaign
- Video story or release
- Other reviewed and graded materials produced for classes

Portfolio standards: Your written work speaks for you and about you. How it appears is a reflection of you. It should be neat, professional and flawless. To achieve that standard, edit it rigorously beyond just spellcheck for grammar and punctuation. In writing for public relations, you must adhere to the *conventions of journalism*. This means you need to follow basic AP style and be *accurate, precise, clear*, and *concise*.

Design: An attractive portfolio will have a consistent graphic look and appear as a "family of materials." This does not mean that you need to invest in professional graphic design. It does mean that you need to create a simple letterhead or stationery style to establish that "family" look. Experiment with simple desktop publishing to find a look to present your work.

Preserve a portfolio: Create a digital portfolio folder for your final, edited, and revised work. In addition, maintain a hard copy portfolio to accompany you to live interviews. Make sure your very best writing samples are easily accessed for immediate transmission.

Professional review: Identify a professor or working professional to review your portfolio to make sure it reflects only the most positive picture of your work.

Share your writing: Your portfolio is only one part of the overall persona you present to the working world. Take time to build not only a portfolio but an online persona (see Personal Branding section) where you can share your work, via your website or blog.

Personal Branding and Online Persona

Coke, Nike, Disney, McDonalds and Mercedes Benz are among the most recognizable brands in the world. While branding has long been associated with companies and products, now individuals can cultivate a brand—think Paris Hilton, the Kardashians, or other celebrities like Miley Cyrus, Oprah Winfrey, and Donald Trump.

Through social media and increased connectivity and sharing, virtually everyone has a digital footprint today. A study conducted by AVG in 2010—six years prior to this handbook's publication—found that a child's digital identity typically started at the age of six months old. AVG's 2014 study found that 30 percent of parents surveyed had shared images of their babies prior to birth from ultrasound scans.

Whatever you share on the Internet remains on the Internet. That's the message in "What Happens in Vegas, Stays on YouTube" by best-selling author of *Socialnomics*, Eric Qualman (**http://www.socialnomics.net/about-erik-qualman/**). It is a quick but substantive guide to personal brand management.

Personal branding means taking control of your digital or online persona. By taking steps to manage your personal brand, you are taking care of and control of your reputation. What others see about you online is your online persona. You are at a stage now where your online persona will play a significant role as you move through college and enter your professional life. Now is the time to carefully craft your personal brand and online persona. Here's a guide to starting that process.

Step #1: Conduct an audit of your online presence.

In the course **PR & Social Media** (COMM 388) students complete a personal branding assignment. The first step is to conduct an audit of their existing online presence. The "audit" involves a series of steps:

- Google yourself. What comes up? Compare search results on page 1 to results on page 4. . . or 10. Analyze what these search results reflect.

- What information about you is presented? What information about you is missing?

- How are you identified on each social media site? What do the names and images used say about you? How would you characterize these ID's (funny, artsy, etc.)?

- On a scale of 1 to 10, with 10 being the "most active," rate your overall online activity level across all sites. Also describe the frequency (daily, frequent, sporadic, inconsistent, etc.) and style of your behavior.

- How are you linked to others? With which social networks are you identified?

Where do you or your image come up when searching other people?

- Consider your "voice." Review your last 50 tweets, posts, comments, pins, etc. Is there anything others might consider inappropriate language or messages? What does your messaging communicate about you and your interests or attitudes?

- A picture is worth a thousand words: what do your photos, boards, and videos say about you to the world? Could any of these violate copyright?

Step #2: Define your personal brand.

This can be quite challenging: How do you want the world to perceive you? What do you want others to know about you? What positive traits or characteristics would you like to showcase? With which social networks do you want to be associated? The answers to these questions become your personal branding *strategy*.

You do not have to choose whether your online persona is "personal" or "professional." With a smart strategy, you can present yourself online without hurting your work life or your social life. The key is to be aware that everything that appears about you online may impact both.

Step #3: Create a personal website.

Your personal website is like your home base. Here you can present your image, your story, your skills, and accomplishments. All of your other online behaviors should link back to your website.

- Free website hosting sites abound with easy-to-use click and drop navigation. Check out several and select one that fits with your main focus, like whether it features your blog or presents a full site with multiple pages.

- Create or choose an all-purpose headshot of you to use across all of your platforms. This will create a consistent online persona. Most bloggers use a simple, friendly visage that is slightly off center. Choose a photo that you like and is appropriate for business or your social circles.

- Write a one or two sentence description of you, sort of like your slogan or tagline. Social media guru Guy Kawasaki uses a simple one: I empower people.

Step #4: Establish social accounts and connect all to your website.

Choose the social media platforms that fit best with your interests as well as your career goals and connects you to the right audience.

- Pinterest is a good choice, for example, if you are interested in fashion; Twitter is essential for the tech and marketing world; Instagram attracts lifestyle, food, and personalities followers; and, sports fans are found on team and sport specific hangouts.

- Facebook's privacy settings, which can be altered for each individual post, encourage many to use the site primarily for family and friends. Posts can be set as "public" to reach the broadest audience or restricted to smaller networks.

- LinkedIn is considered an essential social medium for professionals, gathering profiles and articles by experts.

- Integrate your accounts by linking them to each other and back to your website.

Step #5: Build relationships.

After all, public relations is all about building and maintaining relationships. Connect to other brands. Join industry specific groups on your sites to connect with others like you and to gain insights into industries in which you are interested. On LinkedIn, for example, you can join debates with groups and pose questions. Join scheduled Twitter Chats by individuals in your fields again to gain insights but also to build your Twitter network.

Step #6: Build your brand carefully.

Take your time. You don't need to do all of this in one day. You should get started early in your college years and use your strategy to develop the online persona you want, rather than the one that the Internet will simply reveal.

- Add material to your website throughout your academic career but do so carefully. Be selective about what you put on the site. Keep it interesting and on strategy.

- Make "flawless" your standard. Edit for accuracy and clarity. Edit for punctuation and spelling. Be sure to attribute appropriately to authoritative sources. Follow basic AP style.

- Reflect a range of skills. Show that you can write concisely, as in a 140 character tweet, as well as a 1,000 word in-depth backgrounder.

- Reflect a range of interests. Demonstrate your passion but avoid appearing one-dimensional. You may enjoy all things sports-related but allow the online world to know that you enjoy other things as well, including your hobbies and extracurricular activities.

A Guide to Positions in Public Relations, Advertising, and Marketing from Mason Career Services

Public relations involves shaping how the consumer, the competition, the international community, and the average person on the street view a client. Through a variety of tactics, public relations builds and maintains mutually-beneficial relationships between an organization and its publics. It is a strategic communication process.

Advertising creates and positions brands through paid messages across all media. Advertising agencies act like a marketing consultant, helping the client with all aspects of marketing their product or service, from strategy and concept through execution.

Marketing involves taking a product with specific features and benefits, creating pricing and promotional strategies, and managing the methods that will be used to bring it to market. Marketers create, manage, and enhance products and services so that they reflect well on the company's brand.

Job Functions

PR Coordinator/Account Executive

- Most people enter PR as an account coordinator or, if you go into communications at a company, a PR coordinator. Generally the account coordinator plays an administrative role, supporting an account executive.

- The work involves projects such as monitoring media coverage, assisting in research, creating and maintaining a list of media contacts, and supporting media relations tasks.

Account Supervisor

- A step up from the account executive is the account supervisor. The account supervisor oversees PR accounts, often managing the account executives and account coordinators.

- They often do hands-on executorial work similar to that handled by the account executive, but they'll oversee other staff members assigned to the account as well.

Public Relations Specialists

- This title generally refers to an in-house position managing public relations for an organization.

- Specialists make sure programs are created to match public attitudes, ensuring an organization is publicly embraced.

Media Relations Manager

- Media relations experts pitch ideas for stories. Their job is to convince reporters, bloggers, and citizen journalists to write a story relating to a client.
- Many agencies have full-time positions for people who have honed the skills required to pitch stories to the media.

Social Media Manager

- An evolving position, social media managers are responsible for creating and maintain social accounts like Facebook, Twitter, LinkedIn, and others.
- This position may refer to jobs in an agency or in-house for a company.
- Social media managers are also responsible for monitoring the social conversation regarding their client and industry.
- Senior social media managers may also be tasked with reputation management on social media.

Advertising Account Manager

- Positions range from Assistant Account Executive or Coordinator to senior level Account Supervisor and Director.
- Lower level account managers help direct the day-to-day creation and production of advertising.
- Senior level account managers are responsible for creating campaigns, overall brand management, client relations, proposals, and budgeting.

Advertising Media Planners and Buyers

- They are responsible for making many choices affecting the delivery of the campaign message to the consumer.
- They prepare media buying recommendations to achieve specific reach and frequency of ad messages across all media.

Copywriters, Illustrators, and Creative Professionals

- They create advertisements.
- They are responsible for drawing storyboards, writing copy, designing headlines and body copy, creating slogans, and producing print, broadcast and digital ads.

Traffic and Production Managers

- Working in cooperation with exterior advertising producers, production managers guarantee that each advertisement is completed on deadline and delivered to scheduled media.
- They are employed in-house or often work for production houses that contract services.

Market Research Analysts

- Market researchers serve public relations, marketing, and advertising agencies and departments with qualitative and quantitative research studies.

- These studies are used to test messages, gain attitude and opinion data, and to measure program effectiveness.

Marketing Executive / Junior Marketing Assistant / Marketing Assistant

- Helps the department with the day to day tasks, promotion to this role is generally from within an organization or in some environments, graduates occupy such roles.

Marketing Coordinator / Marketing Officer

- This position involves conducting or arranging market research, working directly with creative agencies, organizing events or promotional campaigns such as literature for product launches.

- Most Marketing Officers/Coordinators report directly to a product or marketing manager.

Product Manager / Senior Product Manager / Group Product or Category Manager

- Dependent on company size the Product Manager may have only one product or many, with the Category Managers being responsible for the entire group of products that his or her team market.

- These roles are most often specific to companies that market products.

Marketing Manager

- This role can be a position in a one-person team or can also be the position which is responsible for teams from 3-10 staff.

- The marketing manager in the smaller company may do every role from assistant through to manager, or in larger companies they manage the junior management-level marketers.

- Note that one would not normally describe a category manager with a marketing budget of £5m as a junior marketer.

How to Get Started

1. Join a student relevant student organization such as AMA student chapter, PRSSA

2. Get involved in the organization as an officer and handle tasks relevant to job functions in which you are interested (e.g. marketing events)

3. Do at least one internship, co-op or job relevant to your industry of interest before graduation

4. Join a professional association related to your industry of interest, such as AAAA, AMA or PRSA. (See *Associations Unlimited (Encyclopedia of Associations)*—access through Mason Libraries; for more information visit **http://infoguides.gmu.edu/c.php?g=120569&p=786042.**)

Communication Job Fairs

The campus chapters of the **Public Relations Student Society of America** and the **Society of Professional Journalists** host a Communication Job Fair annually, usually during the **spring semester**.

The career fair is designed specifically for students in communication, journalism, marketing, and related fields. Participating companies include public relations and advertising agencies, integrated digital firms, public affairs and issues management, and a variety of marketing companies and corporate communication divisions.

At the career fair, students have the chance to speak directly with staff about job and internship opportunities and to learn more about each organization.

"I was one of the first ones to arrive at the Career Fair so I made it around to every table in the room. I brought dozens of resumes, business cards, and my portfolio. I made some solid contacts and received several inquiries. No, I didn't win my first job there, but it really opened my eyes to the job search process. Also, it was a great opportunity to dress and feel like a young, aspiring professional."

A'Darien Johnson, Class of 2015, Communications/IS Sector, Northrop Grumman Corporation

Mason Career Services also hosts career events and job fairs throughout the academic calendar. A major event is held during **fall semester** over two full days with organizations that have internships, co-ops, full-time jobs, and part-time jobs. It is open to all students and alumni of George Mason. It attracts more than 1,200 students each day.

Check the Career Services website (**https://careers.gmu.edu/students/events/fairs/**) to learn about upcoming career events and how you can prepare for a career fair in four easy steps:

- ❧ Research employers
- ❧ Craft your personal pitch
- ❧ Prepare your resume
- ❧ Dress professionally

The PR-Focused Resume

Mason Career Services provides resume-writing workshops and one-on-one guidance on how to prepare and polish your resume. You can also meet with industry-specific counselors who will help you craft a resume that addresses the skills employers seek in an entry-level position in public relations.

Before you begin writing your PR-focused resume, take stock of the skills and experiences you've had during your college years.

- List the PR-specific courses you've taken. Include required and relevant electives.

- Assemble work products from those courses: PR Snapshots, news releases, feature articles, group project reports, and campaign analyses. Review your files for assignments and submissions that demonstrate your skills or knowledge.

- List paid and unpaid internships. Identify *precisely* the type of work you completed and any results you achieved or contributed to.

- List part-time and summer jobs. Do not overstate the "PR-related" aspects of your job as a hostess or landscaper; employers understand that you had to use "people skills" and "time management." Do express precisely any tasks that involved writing, social media, public speaking, event management or media relations.

- List clubs, sports and activities, and your role. Don't overstate your role as fundraiser or publicity chair for your organization. Do express precisely results you may have achieved in that role, i.e., "increased membership from 20 to 75 in three months."

- Identify particular skills developed either through courses or on your own that are in demand in public relations. Also describe your level of proficiency in each. For example, "Experienced in video production," "Intermediate HTML code-writing ability," "Adept at basic desk-top publishing," "Familiar with search engine optimization," or "Amateur photographer."

- Identify specific social media skills, particularly if you are writing a blog, maintaining a website or managing a social site for an organization. Be prepared to describe the strategy you use for this function.

- Include significant course projects that demonstrate hands-on experiences.

The following page provides an example from Mason Career Services of a PR-focused resume:

SAMANTHA PRO
1000 Maple Avenue, Fairfax, VA
703-999-9999
spro@gmail.com

EDUCATION
B.A. in Communication, George Mason University, Fairfax, VA, Expected May 2016
Concentration in Public Relations; Minor in Business GPA 3.58
Relevant Coursework: Principles of PR, PR for Non-Profits, and Marketing in a Global Economy

PROJECTS
Writing for Public Relations client portfolio, Spring 2016: Worked with Mason Cable Network to develop a strategic brand message and create digital materials including a digital brochure, a radio PSA, and a news feature story.

Principles of Public Relations campaign project, Fall 2015: Created and executed a successful campaign to raise funds and participation in the St. Jude annual charity walk, generating 35 walkers, $850 and day-long exposure on a major area radio station and web site.

RELATED EXPERIENCE
Public Relations Intern, Sage Communications, Fairfax, VA   January 2015-Present
- Developed and managed The Starbuck's Festival social media campaign, initiating a 32% increase in web page viewers, a 25% increase in Facebook shares, and a 50% increase in Twitter retweets
- Write and distribute press releases on an as-needed basis
- Organize monthly events for business professionals accommodating over 50 participants at each event

Marketing Intern, Entertainment Industries Council, Reston, VA   May 2014-August 2014
- Researched, developed, and published content for client mailing and company's web-site
- Performed client SWAT analysis to determine strengths and weaknesses
- Aided in analysis of client marketing and advertising strategy; created new promotion plan

ADDITIONAL EXPERIENCE
Peer Advisor, GMU Transition Research Center   August 2015-Present
- Support new students with schedule planning and preparation for faculty advisor meetings during New Student Orientation
- Prepare and facilitate workshops focusing on time management, public speaking, studying, and exam preparation strategies.

ACTIVITIES
Fundraising Chair, GMU Chapter American Marketing Association   August 2014-Present
Member, GMU Chapter Public Relations Student Society of America   August 2013-Present

SKILLS
- Highly skilled in marketing research
- Excellent event management and interpersonal communication skills
- Proficient in social media platforms: Facebook, Twitter, Instagram, Pinterest
- Proficient in Microsoft Office Suite, Adobe Photoshop, and Adobe Final Cut Pro

Information Resources for Students

Public relations practitioners serve as counselors to clients or employers. In that role, practitioners have to monitor current events, issues, and developments that might impact the conduct of business, either immediately, soon or in the future. Students studying public relations should become familiar with a wide variety of sources of information on business, public relations, and integrated digital communication. Here is a list of some of the more popular online sites used by faculty and students. The list is by no means comprehensive but will help lead you in your search. Sites were active at the time of publication but not guaranteed.

Professional organizations in public relations, advertising, and marketing

American Association of Advertising Agencies	www.aaaa.org
American Marketing Association	www.marketingpower.com
Arthur W. Page Society	www.awpagesociety.com
American Society of Association Executives	www.asaecenter.org
Assn. for Education in Journalism & Mass Comm	www.aejmc.org
Association for Women in Communications	www.womcom.org
Association of Government Relations Professionals	www.grprofessionals.org
Business Marketing Association	www.marketing.org
Content Marketing Institute	www.contentmarketinginstitute.com
Institute for PR	www.instituteforpr.org
International Association of Business Communicators	www.iabc.com
International PR Association	www.ipra.org
National Association of Broadcasters	www.nab.org
National Association of Government Communicators	www.nagconline.org
PR Council	www.prcouncil.net
Public Relations Society of America	www.prsa.com
Society for Professional Journalists	www.spj.org
Washington Women in PR	www.wwpr.org
Word of Mouth Marketing Association	www.womma.org

PR News, Blogs, Research, and Resources

PRSA ComPRehension	www.comprehension.prsa.org
Cision	www.cision.com
Forbes	www.forbes.com

Fortune	www.fortune.com
Gallup	www.gallup.com
Holmes Report	www.holmesreport.com
Hootsuite	www.hootsuite.com
Katie D. Payne Measurement	www.painepublishing.com
NYTimes/Business	www.nytimes.com
O'Dwyers	www.odwyerpr.com
Pew Research Center	www.pewresearch.org
Poynter	www.poynter.org
PRAxis	www.prismjournal.org
PR Daily	www.prdaily.com
PR Newswire	www.prnewswire.com
PR Week	www.prweek.com
Social Media Examiner	www.socialmediaexaminer.com
Social Media Today	www.socialmediatoday.com
Social Media Explorer	www.socialmediaexplorer.com
Wall Street Journal	www.wsj.com

Journals of Scholarship in Public Relations and Related Fields

(Note: Access through the University Libraries' website—**http://library.gmu.edu/**—to retrieve articles from these journals.)

Asia Pacific Public Relations Journal, Deakin University, Australia (**https://ojs.deakin.edu.au/index.php/apprj**)

Case Studies in Strategic Communication, University of Southern California, United States (**http://cssc.uscannenberg.org/**)

International Journal of Strategic Communication, International (**http://www.tandfonline.com/toc/hstc20/current**)

Journal of Public Relations Research, Association for Education in Journalism and Mass Communication (AEJMC), United States (**http://www.tandfonline.com/toc/hprr20/current**)

Public Relations Inquiry, Sage Publications, United Kingdom (**http://pri.sagepub.com/**)

Public Relations Journal, Public Relations Society of America, United States (**https://www.prsa.org/Intelligence/PRJournal/index.html**)

Public Relations Review, Elsevier, United Kingdom (**www.journals.elsevier.com/public-relations-review/**)

PRism, Massey University & Bond University, New Zealand (**http://www.prismjournal.org/homepage.html**)

Journal of Communication Management (**http://www.emeraldinsight.com/journal/jcom**)

Corporate Communications: An International Journal (**http://www.emeraldinsight.com/journal/ccij**)

Public Relations and Related Fields Awards & Case Histories

Silver Anvil by PRSA for achievements in public relations (**http://www.prsa.org/Awards/SilverAnvil**)

Clio Awards for achievements in advertising, sports fashion, music, entertainment, and health (**http://www.clioawards.com**)

Webby Awards for excellence on the Internet across websites, mobile, social, advertising, and online film and video (**http://www.webbyawards.com**)

PR Daily Awards in 30 categories including PR on a Shoestring, Infographic, Green Initiative, and Pitch (**http://www.prdaily.com/Main/awards.aspx**)

PRWeek Awards recognizing corporate, agency, nonprofit, and education work in public relations (**http://www.prweek.com/us/awards**)

Digital Communication Awards for achievements, professional campaigning, and strategic thinking in online communications (**http://www.digital-awards.eu**)

MarCom Awards for individuals and companies involved in concept, writing, and design of print, visual, audio and web materials and programs (**http://marcomawards.com**)

European Excellence Awards for achievements in PR and communication (**http://www.excellence-awards.eu**)

Wommy Awards for exceptional word of mouth campaigns (**http://womma.org/wommy-awards/**)

Content Marketing Awards for best content marketing (**http://www.contentmarketingawards.com**)

Writing Resources

Grammar Girl (**http://www.quickanddirtytips.com/grammar-girl**)

The Purdue OWL on Grammar (**https://owl.english.purdue.edu/owl/section/1/5/**)

The Purdue OWL on Associated Press Style (**https://owl.english.purdue.edu/owl/resource/735/02/**)

Grammarly (**https://www.grammarly.com/**)

Jack Lynch: "Guide to Grammar and Style" (**http://andromeda.rutgers.edu/~jlynch/Writing/**)

Speeches.com (**http://speeches.com/**)

Key George Mason University Resources

One-Button Studio—video recording (**http://library.gmu.edu/onebutton/**)

George Mason University Brand Profile—A Guide to Messaging and Visual Identity (**http://brand.gmu.edu/**)

Mason Publishing—Digital publishing services, copyright and scholarly communications, George Mason University Press (**http://publishing.gmu.edu/**)

University Libraries (**http://library.gmu.edu/**)

University Library Research Portal/Strategic Communications (**http://infoguides.gmu.edu/strategiccomm**)

The Writing Center—Tutoring, Workshops, Writing Resources (**http://writingcenter.gmu.edu/**)

University Career Services (**http://careers.gmu.edu/**)

Advice from the Real World:
Mason Alumni Share Advice

Meghan Seeberger, Class of 2015
Account Coordinator, Focused Image

One word: internship. It was a difficult decision to quit my well-paying job during senior year to start an unpaid internship in public relations, but I am so thankful I did. I was able to "test drive" my career and actually witness and apply the knowledge I gained in school. I came away with a true sense of what working in the industry entails—something you just can't get in the classroom. Also, I learned the importance of reading/watching the news and staying up to date with what's going on in the world. While the stories out there may not be the most interesting, knowing about current affairs from different news sources will help you see different styles and perspectives of public relations.

Section II

Developing Key Skills for Public Relations

Advice from the Real World:
Mason Alumni Share Advice

Sandra Whittaker, Senior Digital Producer, Ketchum, Inc.
Fellow, Royal Society for the Encouragement of Arts, Manufactures and
Commerce (the RSA)

Be bold, be hungry, be humble, persevere. The sculptor Michelangelo once said "Every block of stone has a statue inside it, and it is the task of the sculptor to discover it." Sometimes, opportunity is not directly presented to us on a silver platter, it is up to us to chip away, to create that opportunity for ourselves. My path out of college some in our field may say was unorthodox in practice, but I was able to craft my brand by experiencing disciplines and programs that may have not been directly related to PR, but have influenced my "sculpting" greatly. The biggest piece of advice that I can extend: try not to fashion yourself off of someone else's path. Building your own brand and bringing expertise to the table that is refreshing and different will help your career in PR flourish.

Chapter 4

Public Relations' Rules of the Road

Advice from the Real World:
Mason Alumni Share Advice

Tiffany Ngu, Class of 20115
Advertising Services Coordinator, National Rifle Association

My advice is to put forth all of your effort because you will get so much more out of your PR courses than just a letter grade, especially for the group projects. On the job, you have to learn to work with others. Always keep track of your projects and build a portfolio.

Introduction: New Rules, Old Rules, and Rules of the Road

New technologies and social media have altered public relations as it has been practiced over the past 100 years. The foundation of public relations hasn't changed—the building of relationships between organizations and publics—but it is practiced through new and evolving tactics and platforms. In *The New Rules of Marketing and PR*, author David Meerman Scott charts how old practices have changed and how new rules have developed. One of the "old" but still critical rules is Associated Press style. AP style guides how journalists prepare news and how public relations practitioners prepare materials for the news media as well as other audiences. Why? Because PR materials that are AP style-ready when they arrive in a reporter's inbox have a far better chance of being read and used. AP style-ready materials will save the reporter or editor rewriting and editing time. With shrinking media budgets and staffs, well written and AP style-ready PR materials actually help reporters do their job. AP style-written materials are also efficient communications written concisely for clarity.

As you prepare to enter the profession, you need to master the basic "rules of the road" as previewed in this chapter:

- AP Style and the resource text known as the "AP Stylebook"

- Writing that is accurate, precise, clear, and concise

- Using the inverted pyramid structure for news stories

- News characteristics of timely, novel, significance or impact, proximity, prominence, and conflict

- Objective voice and attribution

- Editing and proofing

Tip sheets are included to help you develop a checklist approach to your writing and work in PR.

The Conventions of Journalism and PR

Ever since Ivy Lee penned what's considered the first press release in 1906, media relations has been a core tactic in public relations. For more than 100 years, PR practitioners have relied on journalists and the news media to help their messages reach large audiences. Technology, the Internet, and social media have impacted that dependence. Organizations now have the ability to engage with audiences directly through shared or social media and their owned media, as well as working to generate interest by reporters to write, publish a story and gain "earned media."

This long history and co-dependency has imprinted the *conventions of journalism* upon the public relations business. As a student pursuing a pathway to PR, you will be expected to adhere to these conventions or rules. Your adherence to AP Style is a signal that you are prepared to enter the field of PR.

Associated Press Style: The AP Stylebook guides journalism in the United States. The wire service guide is published annually and is designed to provide consistency in written reports. You should adopt these rules in your writing and refer to the Stylebook for proper treatment for items like date and time; numbers, figures, percent, and money; and works of art. Pay particular attention to the punctuation guide. Errors in AP Style in your writing samples will be a red flag to potential employers or internships. See AP Style Basics in this chapter.

Writing Guidelines: Public relations practitioners follow journalism's approach to news writing and reporting based on these four characteristics:

- **Accurate:** information must be reliable, accurate, and factual
- **Precise:** eliminate anything vague; use detail and evidence to tell the story
- **Clear:** the meaning is unambiguous; the writing can be understood on first reading
- **Concise:** no superfluous words; use only the words necessary to convey the information.

Inverted Pyramid: This convention of journalism guides the structure of a news release. The most important information is positioned at the top with less important presented in descending order of importance. In the inverted pyramid style, the headline, sub-headline, and the first paragraph (or lede) deliver the most important information. A *digital* or *social media* news release uses an inverted pyramid approach but is structured differently. It provides reporters direct links to digital products, like images, video, and audio and links to additional information.

What makes news: Reporters seek stories. What makes news hasn't changed and still involves who, what, when, where, how, and why. Journalists and PR practitioners respect the ingredients of a good story:

- **Novelty:** something new, unusual, novel
- **Prominence:** celebrity, achievement, position
- **Timeliness:** happening now, soon, urgency
- **Proximity:** happening here or nearby
- **Significance/Impact:** what this means to us, how will this affect people?
- **Conflict:** who says what on which side and what does the other side say?

Objective voice: A news release is written in objective voice. It does not speak but offers statements of fact. Use facts, evidence, and credible sources to tell the story.

Attribution: Anything that is not a simple statement of fact should be attributed to a source. An upcoming event could be "much anticipated" according to a previous attendee or a source could comment that it will be "an awesome experience." This will help you avoid overstatement and puffery.

Writing for Public Relations:
AP STYLE BASICS Part #1

1. Dates/months/years/days.

Use figures for dates and years.

Do NOT use st, rd or th with dates.

Capitalize months.

Spell out months, except when using it with a date then it may be abbreviated.

Capitalize days of the week; do not abbreviate.

CORRECT EXAMPLES:

Classes begin Thursday, Aug. 25.

The event will be held Aug. 25, 2013.

The semester begins in January.

2. Time.

CORRECT EXAMPLES:

The event will start at 6 p.m. (NOT 6:00 p.m.)

The alarm went off at 6:30 a.m.

The observance will run from noon to midnight.

3. Titles are capitalized only when preceding the name; lower case after.

CORRECT EXAMPLES:

Secretary of State John Kerry is the guest speaker...

John Kerry, secretary of state, is the guest speaker...

Suzanne Mims, professor of communication, will appear...

Anne Nicotera, chair of the department of communication, said today...

4. Book, movie titles, literary titles.

Use **quotes** for: Books, songs, TV shows, computer games, poems, speeches, works of art.

Do not underline nor italicize.

Capitalize: names of magazines, newspapers or reference materials; do not underline/ italicize.

CORRECT EXAMPLES:

She loves the song "Somewhere Over the Rainbow."
She read it in The Washington Post.

5. Numbers/Quantity.

Never start a sentence with a figure EXCEPT if it is a year.
Spell out numbers under 10; use figures for 10 or more up to 1 million.
For quantities of greater than 999,999: use figure plus million/billion/trillion.
Exception: always use figures for ages.

CORRECT EXAMPLES:

1999 was a great year.
Twenty people lined up for the game.
We had three dogs, nine cats, and 11 ponies.
The pencil cost 5 cents.

More than 100,000 people attended.
The rally drew 2 million people.

6. Ages.

Always use figures.
Hyphenate if the age is an adjective or substitute for a noun.
Don't use apostrophes for ages/age ranges.

CORRECT EXAMPLES:

A 21-year-old student
The girl, 8, stood still.
The student is 21 years old.
He is in his 20s.

7. Money.

Use figures for amounts up to 1 million; then use figure and million/billion/trillion.
Use figures with cents.

CORRECT EXAMPLES:

The pencil cost 5 cents.
He paid $2 for the book. (Not $2.00)

The book cost $20.75.
The yacht sold for $998,000.
The river cleanup cost $1 million.

8. Academic departments are NOT capitalized unless a language.

CORRECT EXAMPLES:

She teaches in the department of communication.
Mary Knox is a professor in the English department.
The student has a double major in accounting and Spanish.
Note: you are NOT a communications major. You are a communication major—singular.

9. Punctuation for quotes.

Commas and periods ALWAYS go inside quotation marks.

CORRECT EXAMPLES:

"I forgot," she said.
"I forgot," she said, "to do my homework."
She said, "I forgot to do my homework."

10. Apostrophe, possessives.

Be careful of singular and plural possessives, contractions.

CORRECT EXAMPLES:

It's quitting time. (Contraction for 'it is.')
The company raised its price.
That dog is hers.
Professor Mims' class ran overtime.
The girls' dresses were blue.
That girl's dress was orange.

Writing for Public Relations:
AP STYLE BASICS Part #2

1. Noun Verb Agreement.

Match the noun and verb (agreement).
Is the noun plural or singular?
Track back to the noun.

EXAMPLES:

Incorrect: The number of the college student suicides are increasing every year.
Track back to the noun: "number" is singular. What verb agrees with it?
Correct: The number of college student suicides is increasing every year.

Incorrect: The benefits of using a single daily dose is significant in terms of patient compliance.
Track back to the noun: "benefits" is plural. What verb agrees with it?
Correct: The benefits of using a single daily dose are significant in terms of patient compliance.

2. Correct word.

Do you confuse any of the words in this list below?
Make sure you know which is the correct word for your use.

- accept, except
- adapt, adept, adopt
- affect, effect
- compliment, complement
- disinterested, uninterested
- stationary, stationery
- implicit, explicit
- ensure, insure, assure
- lose, loose
- proceed, precede
- principal, principle

- passed, past
- regardless, irregardless
- site, sight, site
- there, their

3. Avoid jargon, slang, and clichés.

Craft your sentence for meaning and avoid canned expressions, clichés, and jargon or slang, like the following:

- Putting it out there
- Creating a buzz
- Pleased to announce
- Changed 180 degrees
- He gave it 120 percent
- Discuss this topic off line
- Worked like a charm

4. Reduce wordiness.

Increase clarity by eliminating unnecessary words.

EXAMPLES:

Draft sentence: Being that tomorrow is the day that the career fair is going be held, we were wondering if you could possibly be able to switch the date of the test to another day other than tomorrow?

Less wordy: Will you please consider moving the test to next week? Tomorrow is the career fair and many students are planning to attend.

5. Word choice.

Select the word that best communicates your message.
Use action verbs.
Express precisely.

EXAMPLES:

Draft sentence: He walked toward the policeman.
Stronger verb choice: He stomped angrily toward the policeman.
Stronger verb choice: He ambled slowly toward the policeman.
Stronger verb choice: He marched confidently toward the policeman.

6. Avoid puffery.

Discipline writing to be concrete and credible by avoiding puffery—generalized claims such as:

- Amazing array
- Awesome experience
- The most exciting lineup
- World's best
- Region's finest
- Leading expert

7. Be concrete and credible.

EXAMPLES:

- Voted the #1 restaurant by Washingtonian readers
- Given four stars by TripAdvisor
- Top rating on Yelp
- An expert in medical malpractice who has tried more than 400 cases in the past 30 years
- The theater critic for The New York Times said the lineup of performers is the most star-studded listing seen in the last decade.

Writing for Public Relations:
Rules of the Road

1. Write simple sentences.

- Use simple, tight noun-verb-object construction.
- Shorter is better.
- Make dense with fact.
- Get to the point quickly.
- Keep subject and modifiers together in the sentence.
- Make clear which subject is being modified.
- Avoid multi-word modifiers before noun.
- Pyramid lists by putting smaller words first.

2. Use active voice and present tense.

- Enhances clarity.
- Reduces wordiness.
- Gets to the point quickly.

3. Use only one main idea per paragraph.

- Use topic sentences.
- Avoid long sentences.
- Break out lists into bullet points.
- Use subheads to help guide the reader.
- End paragraph with a transition to the next.

4. Choose words carefully.

- Simple is best.
- Word choice should match the intended audience.
- Seek most precise word.
- Use the correct word.
- Choose words with impact.
- Choose action verbs.

5. Eliminate wordiness.

- Prune your sentences.
- Use fewer words.
- Delete unnecessary words and phrases.
- Eliminate redundancy.
- Eliminate hyperbole.

6. Use simple, clear language.

- Avoid jargon.
- Don't use clichés or trite phrases.
- Don't use slang.
- Recognize and simplify gobbledygook.

7. Provide evidence, not hyperbole, to persuade.

- Build your case with fact.
- Enable your reader to reach the conclusion.
- Don't use puffery.

8. Be specific.

- Delete or clarify any vague descriptions.
- Revise imprecise wording.
- Use data, examples, and comparisons.
- Offer detail but don't overwhelm.

9. Aim for flawless.

- Use spell check.
- Don't rely on spell check.
- Review for grammar, spelling, and punctuation.

10. Edit rigorously.

- Use resources.
- Print and edit.
- Read it aloud and edit.
- Use another set of eyes.

Writing for Public Relations:
Common Problems—Simple Solutions

Problem	Example	Correction
Passive voice vs. active voice. Reduces clarity and increases wordiness.	It was decided by the committee to postpone action on the bill until it could be determined that the availability of funds could be coordinated. **Better:** The committee postponed action on the bill until funds are available.	Use active voice: the subject performs the action expressed in the verb. Look for who is doing what to whom: Passive: The boy was bitten by the dog. Active: The dog bit the boy.
Sentence structure makes meaning unclear or incorrect. A misplaced modifier is usually the culprit.	The proposed budget includes salary increases for faculty earning a positive ranking of 2 percent. **Better:** The proposed budget includes salary increases of 2 percent for faculty earning a positive ranking.	Keep subject and words that modify it together in the sentence. Make it clear which subject is being modified: The girl was crying on the horse. Better: The girl on the horse was crying.
Wordy. Too many words. Not simply stated.	They have assisted numerous companies in the development of a system that can be utilized in the monitoring of their customer service operations. **Better:** They have helped many companies develop systems for monitoring their customer service operations.	Use word savers. Use simpler words. Numerous = many Assisted = helped Utilized = used 23 words vs. 13

Problem	Example	Correction
Word choice is incorrect.	The crowd was visibly effected when the band walked down Pennsylvania Avenue. **Better:** The crowd was visibly affected when the band walked down Pennsylvania Avenue.	Use grammar and spelling tools to help identify incorrect usage. Avoid common incorrect usage: Stationery, stationary principle, principal Cite, sight, site except, accept Ensure, assure, insure its, it's
Word choice is imprecise.	The crowd was visibly affected when the band walked down Pennsylvania Avenue. **Better:** The crowd cheered and applauded when the band marched down Pennsylvania Avenue.	Make your words work. Be specific. Choose words to precisely communicate the action.
Sentence is vague.	The project will involve many organizations as well as several corporate sponsors and is expected to attract numerous celebrities and politicians. **Better:** The project involves about 30 local and national organizations and a dozen corporate sponsors including Lockheed Martin and IBM. Governor Terry McAuliffe, country singer Martina McBride, and other notables are expected to attend.	Be specific. Don't leave the reader asking questions. Give detail. Paint a full picture. Give examples. Identify subjects clearly.
Words are lofty, not simple. Sentence is not concise.	A determination was put forth that the schedule for final exams undergo an alteration for both the days and the actual times of the planned exams. **Better:** The updated final exam schedule revises both the days and times when exams will be held.	Use simple words. Get rid of lofty (put forth, alteration). Use action verbs (revises instead of undergo alteration). Use simple noun-verb-object construction.

Problem	Example	Correction
Lack of clarity. Poor sentence structure. Incomplete information. More detail is needed to paint a fuller picture	The breastfeeding sessions by the local agency are in conjunction with a national program for mothers and their babies to be held next week. **Better:** An information session on breastfeeding will be held May 7. Mother are invited to attend with their babies for the free education and training program. The local program is in conjunction with national efforts by the Office on Women's Health of the Department of Health and Human Services.	Answer all of the questions a reader might have. Add detail. Be specific.
Jargon reduces clarity.	Finalists are urged to discuss final submission procedures with the committee offline. **Better:** Finalists should call 703-555-1212 to discuss final submission procedures. Do not use email.	Don't use jargon or insider terms. Choose words that precisely communicate your meaning to a broad audience.
Spelling error.	The new secretary lead a busy life during her decades-long tenure at the Gates Foundation. **Better:** The new secretary led a busy life during her decades-long tenure at the Gates Foundation.	Don't rely on spell check. Reading aloud often helps catch this type of common mistake.

Problem	Example	Correction
Awkward phrasing. Message is jumbled. Lack of clarity	Quinoa really began to rise around 2008 and is steadily gaining traction as some South American farmers begin to only farm quinoa and researchers in America are beginning study how to grow quinoa in the U.S. **Better:** Quinoa sales have been steadily rising since 2008, when the product became more popular with Americans. Researchers and farmers in the United States are studying how to grow the product here. Sales are high enough now that South American farmers are moving toward quinoa-only farms.	Read aloud to yourself, slowly Listen to how this sounds, then rewrite.
Trite phrases are imprecise and reduce clarity.	The oil giant has managed to stay ahead of the game due to its highly disciplined corporate culture that encourages teams to think outside the box. **Better:** The oil giant's continued success is due to a disciplined corporate culture that resists mediocrity and encourages creative problem solving.	Don't use clichés or trite phrases. Be specific. Be precise. Contribute more detail.
Hyperbole weakens credibility.	The weekend event includes an amazing schedule of exciting events that will thrill parent and child alike! **Better:** The weekend event includes activities for both children and their parents, ranging from pony rides to pumpkin carving. "My family just loves this event. We come every year, rain or shine," said the 35-year-old mother of three.	Use facts to persuade. Don't exaggerate or overstate. Use quotes from others as evidence.

Tip Sheet:
Rules for Pre-editing and Editing

1. Complete pilot's checklist.

- ❧ Define purpose.
- ❧ Gather information, research.
- ❧ Understand to whom you are writing.
- ❧ Consider for whom you are writing.
- ❧ Define desired outcome.
- ❧ Define your call to action.
- ❧ Anticipate the reader's questions.

2. Define your message strategy.

- ❧ How will you present key points?
- ❧ Consider best approaches (cognitive, affective, conative).
- ❧ Write to stay on message.

3. Pre-edit.

- ❧ Complete pilot's checklist.
- ❧ Choose a message strategy.
- ❧ Outline by paragraph.
- ❧ Determine length.
- ❧ Choose what NOT to include.
- ❧ Set a deadline.
- ❧ Plan when/how to rewrite.

3. Edit for content.

- ❧ Pause. Think about something else. Refresh.
- ❧ Checklist for content:
  - Does it make sense?

- Will the intended reader understand?
- Is it coherent?
- Is anything vague?
- Anything missing? Unanswered?
- Is there a call to action? A next step?
- Are you using the proper tone?
- Did you stay on message?

4. Edit for flawless.

- Print it out and edit by hand.
- Read it aloud.
- Edit for the 10 rules of the road.
- Prune your sentences. Edit unnecessary words.
- Look twice at word choice: is it the best word? The most precise word?
- Check for flow: do you have topic sentences? Transitions?
- Use resources.
- Use a fresh pair of eyes.
- Rewrite. Finalize.

5. Rules of Editing.

- Always plan to rewrite.
- Meet your deadlines.
- Always use but don't rely on spell check.
- Insist on error-free.
- Satisfy your professional standards:
  - Accurate
  - Precise
  - Clear
  - Concise

Writing Self-Diagnosis

Despite what Shakespeare's mother must have thought, no one is born a great writer. Is writing a skill that can be learned? Is it nature or nurture? Faulkner said he first believed that it was an innate talent. He later reconsidered and said it wasn't talent but mere patience that resulted in good writing. What are the traits that create strong writing?

One answer is time. Good writing takes time, a precious commodity for most on-the-job writing. Often you have far less time to compose than you need. Learning to write *efficiently* will help you produce better writing within short timeframes.

How do you increase the efficiency of your writing process? The answer lies in:

- Understanding how you write
- Acknowledging your weaknesses
- Using your strengths
- Being deliberate about good writing and editing
- Adhering slavishly to standards

Use this self-diagnosis tool to assess your writing skills and then commit to tackling weaknesses. Developing strong writing skills is one of the best investments you can make in your future as you travel the PR pathway.

Self-Diagnosis

Question: How do you write? What process do you use? There are many writing methods. What is yours?

- **James Joyce:** I just sit down and write. I use a stream-of-consciousness approach where I put it all down and write until I don't have anything left to say. Then I edit, rearrange, edit, and rewrite until I'm satisfied.

- **J.K. Rowling:** I plan. I outline my thoughts and write from start to finish.

- **Oprah Winfrey:** I talk through my message before I write. I like to articulate my thoughts first.

- **Stephen King:** I use a hybrid: a rough outline plus writing freely to get it down on paper; then I edit rigorously.

- **Maurice Sendak:** My method is a bit different…

Question: What is your basic writing style? Do any of these descriptions sound like you?

- **The Jumbler:** too many ideas cloud the main message; sentences end up ambiguous or vague. I often rewrite to clarify the primary idea.

- **A High Calorie Writer:** too many words; sentences are too long; the draft is too long, overflowing with ideas. I often rewrite to shorten the piece and be more concise.

- **The Jack Sprat Syndrome:** too brief; too terse; not enough explanation or detail. I often rewrite to add material for more precise meaning.

- **A Slow Cooker:** trouble getting started and/or takes a long time to write the first draft. I just can't get started or it seems to take me longer than others to complete writing tasks.

- **A Preacher:** messaging is overdone; too lofty; sermonizing. I often rewrite to use simpler words and be more direct.

- **Lady GaGa?**....my weaknesses don't fit the above molds exactly. My style is more....

Question: A variety of maladies afflict writing. For you, which area needs the most attention?

- Sloppy mistakes—missing words, misspellings, wrong words, overlooked punctuation

- Grammar—unsure about certain usage like noun-verb agreement, prepositional phrases, pronouns, that/which, who/whom, apostrophes, and possessives

- Punctuation—always have a problem with (commas, semicolons, quotes...)

- Adhering to AP style—need to become more familiar

- Clarity—need to improve writing so that the meaning is unambiguous

- Brevity—need to get to the point quickly and be more concise

- Word choice—need to choose better words for more precise meaning

- Wordiness—need to edit out unnecessary words

- Sentence structure—need sentences to be simpler and shorter

- Tone—need to moderate or enliven my style

- Formalize—need to relax or enhance formality

- Humanize—need to add more examples and comparisons

- Call to action—need my message to move the reader to the next step

- Plan—need to gather all material before I write

- Deadlines—need to set my own deadlines in order to meet the deadline

- Organize—need better organization overall

Question: What is your editing routine? Editing is sometimes a luxury for on-the-job writers but you always edit in some way. How do you edit?

- I edit as I go. I often rewrite and rewrite a sentence until it's perfect.
- I complete the draft and then edit it, line-by-line and sentence-by-sentence.
- I edit it and then usually have someone else read it.
- I read it (whisper it) out loud to "hear" my errors.
- I print it, read it, edit, and rewrite.
- My method of editing is a bit different...

Question: What issues do you have when editing?

- I don't have enough time.
- It takes me forever.
- I can't stop editing.
- I just don't see my mistakes.
- I see what's wrong but unsure how to fix it.
- I get attached to my phrasing and don't want to delete.
- I am not used to the Associated Press Style Manual.

Chapter 5

The PR Tool Box

Advice from the Real World:
Mason Alumni Share Advice

Mariam Aburdineh, Class of 2013
Writer/Editor, The Wolf Trap Foundation for the Performing Arts

Don't underestimate your class projects. Several professors assign meaningful projects that can be listed on your resume. If you helped a specific client or got something published, list it! Just because you worked on it in class doesn't mean it's not real experience. Talk to your professors and develop professional connections with them. In my case, going to office hours gave me that opportunity and helped me realize the importance of doing so in general.

The Public Relations Tool Box

Many professionals make use of a toolbox. Doctors, carpenters, golfers, and salesman all have tools that help them do their job. What would a doctor be without a stethoscope or thermometer? How does a three handicapper win golf tournaments without a putter? These tools enable the professionals to not only do their job but also do it successfully. Public relations professionals also have a set of tools from they can use to build relationships and engage with media and other publics. Instead of a stethoscope or a putter, PR practitioners use specific tools, described in this chapter, ranging from media advisories and pitch letters to Facebook pages, websites, and social media accounts. These tools help PR people send strategic messages to their publics, like investors, news media, elected officials, other influencers, customers, and consumers.

Tools like press releases, videos, podcasts, Slideshare stacks, whitepapers, backgrounders, feature articles, blogs, and other social media content (and more) need to be in your personal toolbox. Take the time now, in college, to learn how to create these tools and practice producing them. Try out free desktop publishing that will add images to your tweets and explore creating a website with one of the many free hosting sites. Experiment with video production and promoting what "Contagious" author Jonah Berger calls valuable virality. This adaptability and willingness to try new approaches and master them will make you attractive in the workplace. Start by mastering the basic tools, like a press release and fact sheet, and expand from there to using the latest technologies and platforms and apps to communicate *strategically* and *efficiently*.

PR Tools

- **The News Release:** This particular vehicle (originally called a "Press Release") may be the oldest in the public relations worker's toolbox. Is it dead, as declared by Coca Cola and other major organizations? It is not dead, according release and usage numbers by PRNewswire, BusinessWire, and other news distribution services, but it is different. A news release is no longer trying to reach or influence solely established journalists but the broader audience of traditional media, bloggers, online publications, citizen journalists, and general social media.

- **Social Media Release:** These releases are a streamlined, quick read digital version of the traditional news release, often with digital images, video, and audio. While the traditional news release presents a full story, this version provides the main elements of a hard news story—who, what, when, where, how, and why—and often will list quotes with sources as well as links to other sources of information.

- **Fact Sheets:** Usually a "one sheet" that serves as an all-in-one summary of the key pieces of information any audience might seek about a client. It is often the cornerstone of a full set of materials found in the traditional "press kit."

- **Backgrounders:** This is an in-depth paper that pulls together substantive research and commentary on an issue.

- **Blogs:** At anywhere from 250 to 1000 words, blog posts have to be relevant, substantive, and offer practical value. People search the Internet for information to solve some type of problem or inquiry. A good blog post solves the problem.

- **Media Kits:** Originally, this kit was created for the working news media and is still used to help working journalists prepare news or feature stories. It includes a basic fact sheet as well as other materials that provide additional data, research, trends, statistics, and commentary relating to the client and industry. Today, a full media or press kit is usually digital and can be found on an organization's website under "news room."

- **Email Pitch:** This is a concise effort sent via email to persuade a reporter to write about your story, relying on a clear subject line and a short argument for why this story is of interest.

In this chapter you will find examples of student work on assignments you are likely to have in your PR courses. Be inspired by their work but don't treat these examples like a template. You want to develop your personal approach to writing; don't inhibit your creativity by following a template precisely.

The News Release

The news release (or press release, as it was originally called) may be the oldest item in PR toolbox. A rough estimate by *PR Daily* of the number of news releases issued daily by only *PRNewswire*, *BusinessWire*, and *Marketwire* was 1,759 per day, or 642,000 during all of 2013. The news release is not dead, despite being declared so recently by Coca Cola and other major organizations. While still very much alive, however, the press release is different. It is no longer intended merely for the established, working media but is now directed to a much broader audience that includes traditional media, bloggers, online publications, citizen journalists, and general social media.

The standard press release includes several ingredients or elements. These include the lede or lead paragraph, the body of the text itself, and usually ends with a boilerplate or a standard description of the organization and how to obtain further information. Writers have their own system for drafting a release but generally follow these steps:

1. Write the headline. Add a subhead with added detail. If the reader only makes it through the headlines and the first paragraph, you've succeeded in communicating your most important information.

2. Write the lead (lede). One to three sentences. Present the WHAT. Add context, the WHY.

3. Add details, facts: when, where, who, how.

4. Use quote to add interest.

5. Attribute information to authoritative source.

6. Additional detail, as needed.

7. Boilerplate: standard text, such as information about the company.

The lede, or lead paragraph, should be written *strategically* to highlight the most newsworthy characteristics of the message but there is more than one way to craft the lead. On the following two pages, take a look at student examples of lead paragraphs from news releases announcing Mason's annual communication symposium. Then, review the traditional news release issued by the Insight Committee. Finally, consider the social media or digital news release version for the same event.

The Lede/Lead Paragraph: Student Examples

News Release

FOR RELEASE: October 20, 2015   **CONTACT: Karlene Koh, 123-456-7890**
email@email

CONTENT MARKETING SYMPOSIUM

Explore the power of storytelling by networking with PR professionals

(Fairfax, VA – October 20) — The George Mason University Department of Communication is hosting its fifth annual communication forum October 20 from 9:30 a.m. to 1 p.m. in Dewberry Hall in the Johnson Center. Sponsored by the Insight Committee of the George Mason University Department of Communication, "Content Marketing: The Art of Storytelling Across Media Platforms" will consist of a keynote address, a panel discussion, and a speed mentoring session. At this event, students will have the opportunity to network and interact directly with communication professionals who will help guide them to their future career.

News Release

FOR IMMEDIATE RELEASE   **Contact: Ace Chapman, email@email**
Ph: 123-456-7890

George Mason students have the opportunity to learn from industry professionals

(Fairfax, Virginia – September 23, 2015) — Mason students will have the opportunity to attend a conference discussing content marketing, one of the current topics on the leading edge in the communications industry.

"Be knowledgeable about the business of media," says Tara Ruszkowski, currently the CEO of Ruszkowski & Associates, LLC, a public affairs and communications practice, based in Vienna. She also serves as a member of the Mason communication department's Insight Committee, which serves as a volunteer advisory board to the department that provides students access to advice and events including this year's Student/Industry Communications Forum.

News Release

FOR IMMEDIATE RELEASE

CONTACT: Lori Lawson, (123) 456-7890
email@email

FIFTH ANNUAL CAREER SYMPOSIUM BRINGS
INDUSTRY LEADERS TO MASON STUDENTS

Speed mentoring offers unique access to communication professionals

(Fairfax, Va. – Oct. 19) — On Tuesday, Oct. 20, the Insight Committee and George Mason University's Department of Communication will hold the fifth annual Career Symposium from 9:30 a.m. to 12:45 p.m. in Dewberry Hall on the Fairfax Campus. The free event presents a unique opportunity for students interested in public relations and marketing to interact closely with industry leaders as they discuss the latest trends in content marketing and storytelling.

2015 GMU Student/Industry Communications Forum

An annual event sponsored by The Insight Committee of The Department of Communication

FOR IMMEDIATE RELEASE   Contact: Mike Dickerson 571-228-3967

October 20 Forum on Content Marketing Features Student Access to Communications Industry Experts

Keynote Kathryn McCarthy, Chairman & CEO of ThinkGeek and GeekNet, Complemented by Panel of Industry Leaders

(Fairfax, VA – October 9, 2015) — Focused on the fastest-growing segment of communications today, the Insight Committee of the George Mason University Department of Communication is hosting its 5th annual Communication Forum for students on October 20, 2015: **"Content Marketing: The Art of Storytelling Across Media Platforms."** The event is being held from 9:30 a.m. to 1:00 p.m. at the Johnson Center, Lower Level, Dewberry Hall. Included in the program is a unique opportunity for participating students to rotate to "speed mentors" where they can interact directly with communications professionals.

Associate Professor of Communications Michael Dickerson cites the *Columbia Journalism Review* definition of content marketing as including "essentially any form of content (a Facebook post, a celebrity Q&A, a feature-length documentary) created on or behalf of a brand with the hope that it will attract an audience on its own merits—as opposed to traditional advertising, which has the far smaller ambition of gaining notice from a captive audience before the ad break ends, or the page gets flipped, and the real content begins."

Specifics of the program include:

9:30 a.m. – 9:50 a.m. Introductions & Defining Content Marketing

Michael Meyer, senior writer, *Columbia Journalism Review*

9:50 a.m. – 10:30 a.m. Keynote address

Kathryn McCarthy, chairman & CEO, ThinkGeek and GeekNet

10:35 a.m. – 11:30 a.m. Panel discussion

Bill Aydelott, director-producer-cameraman, Waverly Motion Pictures, LLC

Gary Goldhammer, storyteller and digital communications strategist, H&K Strategies

Linda Smith, digital marketing strategist, Sage Communications

Kathryn McCarthy, chairman & CEO, ThinkGeek and GeekNet

11:30 a.m. – 1:00 p.m. Speed mentoring Q&A session with students

An annual event, the Student/Industry Communications Forum is sponsored by The Insight Committee, a volunteer advisory board to the Communication Department. The committee is comprised of leaders in communication in the Washington, D.C. area and is chaired by Tom Hoog, vice chairman, Hill+Knowlton Strategies.

For more information on the event, contact Mike Dickerson, 571-228-3967

###

Digital News Release: Student Example

GEORGE
MASON Communication
UNIVERSITY COLLEGE OF HUMANITIES AND SOCIAL SCIENCES

Fifth Annual Career Symposium Brings Industry Leaders to Mason Students

19 Oct. 2015

On Tuesday, Oct. 20, the Insight Committee and George Mason University's Department of Communication will hold the fifth annual Career Symposium from 9:30 a.m. to 12:45 p.m. in Dewberry Hall on the Fairfax Campus. The free event presents a unique opportunity for students interested in public relations and marketing to interact closely with industry leaders as they discuss the latest trends in content marketing and storytelling.

Prior to a keynote address by Kathryn McCarthy, chairman and CEO of online retailer ThinkGeek and GeekNet, participants will hear opening remarks from:

- **Anne Nicotera**, chair, George Mason University's Department of Communication
- **David Wu** provost and executive vice president, George Mason University
- **Tom Hoog**, Chairman, Hill+Knowlton Strategies, Inc.
- **Gary Goldhammer**, storyteller and digital communications strategist, Group SJR

The event will then feature a panel with high-level representatives from:

- **Tom Hoog**, Chairman, Hill+Knowlton Strategies, Inc.
- **Linda Smith**, digital marketing strategist, Sage Communication
- **Bill Aydelott**, director-producer-cameraman, Waverly Motion Pictures, LLC.
- **Gary Goldhammer**, storyteller and digital communications strategist, Group SJR

CONTACTS

Client
Department of Communication
George Mason University

✉ anicoter@gmu.edu
☎ (703) 993-1090
🐦 @MasonCommDept
🌐 communication.gmu.edu

Agency
Lori Lawson
Mims PR

✉ llawson@gmu.edu
☎ (757) 715-0800
🐦 @l_x_3
🌐 wearemimspr.com

MULTIMEDIA

Livecast

- **Kathryn McCarthy**, chairman and CEO, GeekNet

Participants will also have the opportunity to network in small groups with industry professionals as part of a speed mentoring session.

"Sometimes, in a room of 400 or 500 people, it can be hard to put your hand up," states Mason's Department of Communication Director of Outreach Michael Dickerson. "But," he continues, "if you're sitting across the table from a few other students, it is much easier and much more relaxed."

To obtain a schedule of events or to learn more about special guests, visit http://communication.gmu.edu/events/5548 or contact the Department of Communication at (703) 993-1096.

PHOTOS FROM PREVIOUS SYMPOSIUM

###

Event Flyer

KEYWORD CLOUD

MORE INFORMATION

George Mason University
Department of Communication

The Insight Committee

Press Release

2014 Forum

News Release Template

WeArePR
Intro/Principles of Public Relations
Careers start here.

FOR RELEASE: (insert date or "Immediate")   **CONTACT: (Your name, email & Cell)**

HEADLINE should be centered. Use initial caps.

SUBHEAD that adds more detail is not required but is often helpful.

(Fairfax, VA – August 28 – this is the DATELINE) Begin your text after the dateline. Always use business stationery of the organization issuing the release; for example, this news release template uses the stationery for a section of COMM 204/330. Your final draft will be single-spaced; academic assignments may ask for double-spacing to aid editing. Use Times New Roman in 12 pt. Indent your paragraphs just three spaces.

In your first paragraph, include key facts that explain the most important information —usually the "what"—and provide some context for why it is news. Use just a few sentences. Make this paragraph an umbrella under which other facts fall. Include additional information in descending order of importance.

Add more facts and details in descending order of importance to your audience. "Classes will be canceled Wednesday" may not be that important to the general population but would be very important to Mason students and should be fairly high up or in the subhead.

Include quotes to add human interest. Do not use quotes for simple factual information.

Avoid wordiness. Use simple phrasing. Read your draft aloud to "hear" mistakes.

News releases don't "speak;" news releases can't state "it will be awesome," or "you don't want to miss this event." Anything that is not a simple statement of fact should be attributed to someone. Write your release so others conclude, "it will be awesome."

If you continue on to a second page, use   --- more   at the bottom right.

At the end of the release, put three number symbols, centered.

###

Editing the News Release

WeArePR
Intro/Principles of Public Relations
Careers start here.

EDITING CHECKLIST

PROPER FORMAT: Use news release stationery, include *For Release, Contact information.* Center the headline and use dateline to start first paragraph.

HEADLINE: A headline grabs your attention and communicates information—it is not a simple "title." A subhead is preferred; the two together do most of the job of the release.

LEDE/LEAD PARAGRAPH: In a hard news release, the basic facts and most newsworthy aspect should be in the first paragraph. In a "soft" news feature approach, it is permissible for the key facts to be in the second paragraph.

UMBRELLA: Does the headline and/or first paragraph provide an "umbrella" under which the rest of the story stands? Does it provide a good summary of what your release is about?

INVERTED PYRAMID: Generally, is the information presented in descending order of importance?

ATTRIBUTION: Anything that is not a statement of fact must be attributed to a source. This can be quoted directly or indirectly.

QUOTES: Are sources quoted? Quotes help tell the story and help humanize the release.

SOURCES IDENTIFIED: Are sources fully identified? Upon first reference, identify the source by full name, title if applicable or other information that establishes the source's context to the story.

ANYTHING MISSING: Do you have questions after reading this? Is it thorough? Is it precise and accurate?

PROPER AP STYLE: Have you used proper AP style for titles, date, time, money...?

FOLLOW ALL THE RULES: Is this accurate? Is it precise and presented with facts? Is it clear and unambiguous? Is it concise without unnecessary words?

SLOPPY OR ERROR FREE: Nothing is worse than misspellings, poor grammar, and improper punctuation. Edit and proofread. Edit and proofread again.

The Fact Sheet

Social media have changed many aspects of public relations. The need for basic tools like a fact sheet has not changed. A fact sheet is a simple document that presents key facts and information about an organization, product or issue at a glance. An effective fact sheet is one that answers all of the basic questions in an easy-to-read and quick-read format. ***Review how well the fact sheet supports the news release in the student example for Mason Cable on the following pages.***

For the fictitious MasonCakes campus bakery, you would create a list of items to include as follows:

Content

Content matters most. Be thorough; answer all questions. Be concise; eliminate wordiness. Be specific; choose words carefully.

- Definition in brief: a 1-2 sentence description that succinctly states the organization and its primary mission.
  - *MasonCakes is a student-owned bakery and purveyor of fun, tasty, and all-natural treats. Our goal is to become the favorite gift and self-reward for everyone on campus.*
- Cupcake standard offerings
- Cupcake special event, holiday offers
- Cupcake custom orders
- Pricing: single orders, multiple cakes, by the dozen, for a party
- Gift options (birthdays, engagements, congrats)
- Packaging options
- Delivery options
- How to order
- Testimonials
- Guarantee (satisfaction)
- Location: address, map
- Contact: website address, phone number

- Owners: names, contact info
- Social: icons w/ links to Facebook, Twitter, etc.

Images

A picture is worth a thousand words, it really is. Use images to help create your brand and to communicate your values. Select images to support your strategy, as noted in your definition in brief.

- Cupcake varieties (colorful and fun)
- Customized cupcake (your offerings)
- Owner/baker (help communicate student-owned)
- Owner/baker (humanize, put a face with the brand)
- Packaging (show cupcakes as gifts)
- Customer (humanize; makes testimonial credible)
- Mason logo and/or statue (support "institution" goal)

Layout

Look at dozens of fact sheets before you begin your layout. White space helps the reader move across the page. Use the space you have carefully; do not overwhelm. Discard text or reduce it to a brief identifier when an image communicates your message. Use text boxes and columns to help organize your material.

Design

You may find design help right on your computer, in PowerPoint or Word. Try experimenting with free desktop publishing. While it may be challenging at first, trial and error usually paves the way to confident design. An effective fact sheet is one that is content-rich in an easy to read format.

Fact Sheet 10-Point Checklist

1. Key facts: Use full and correct name, street address, email address, telephone, cell number, social media links/icons and, if appropriate, fax number, small map/link.

2. Operating facts: Show the full range of services or products offered, publics served, mission, hours of operation, pricing.

3. Branding: Is client brand/logo/image included (or been created)?

4. Positioning: Is client "positioned" in the marketplace i.e. "woman owned firm," "entrepreneurial venture," "independently owned and operated," "largest supplier of xx in the metro area."

5. Graphic layout and design: Are the layout and graphics pleasing? Too busy or not busy enough? Coherent or erratic? Enough white space? Does the look support the brand? Interesting? Attention-getting? Legible? Or...boring?

6. Images: The brain processes images 60,000 times faster than text! Select images to replace words and eliminate text-heavy section.

7. References/Testimonials: Do you have references or testimonials from clients or customers? Awards, "best of" lists, excerpts from news articles or reviews.

8. Complete: Don't leave the reader asking questions. Is it thorough and accurate? Is it clear and precise? Don't leave in any vague or confusing statements.

9. Humanizing tactics: Show real people running a real business. Use photos or quotes.

10. Professional appearance: As a whole, does it represent the client accurately and positively?

News Release and Fact Sheet: Student Example

Mason Cable Network
Your Face. Your Voice.

FOR RELEASE: Immediate   CONTACT: Ashley Hill, email@email
123-456-7890

Mason Cable Network Hosts Day Long Event for George Mason Students
MCN Is Giving Away Prizes Leading Up To MCN Takeover

(Fairfax, VA – March 27, 2015) – At George Mason University on April 17, Mason Cable Network, the student run campus television station, is hosting a 12-hour special event on channel 231 for the GMU student body.

Mason Cable Network is inviting all students as well as faculty and staff to come together and enjoy a stress free day at the end of the spring semester by joining in watching MCN Takeover. Airing from 12 p.m. to 12 a.m., this all day event will cater to a diverse group of people by debuting a variety of student created shows, airing two well known movies at the end of the night, and giving students the chance to win prizes all throughout the day.

Leading up to the MCN Takeover, Mason Cable Network will hold multiple events to raise awareness of the day. This campus network will engage students in different activities such as sharing a cup of lemonade with Mason Cable Network, a contest to test students' knowledge of GMU in the North Plaza on campus, and a chance to be in a video that captures the essence of GMU. For a complete list of events, the schedule for MCN Takeover can be found online on Mason Cable Network's Twitter, Facebook, and Instagram page.

"MCN Takeover is going to be a great opportunity for students alike to join together and relax after a long year. It not only brings the student body together through common interests but also provides an outlet for everyone to reduce his or her level of stress," says Robert Horan, the general manager of Mason Cable Network.

--- more

Mason Cable Network is George Mason University's student operated on campus television station. MCN airs on the local Fairfax channel 231 24/7 to approximately 6,000 residents. Geared towards George Mason students, MCN produces live shows, pre-recorded shows, and student projects. MCN has been providing students with entertainment and news for over 10 years.

For more information visit MasonCableNetwork.com or contact Ashley Hill at ahill17@gmu.edu

###

Mason Cable Network

Your Face. Your Voice.

About Us

Mason Cable Network is George Mason University's student operated on campus television station. MCN airs on the local Fairfax channel 231 24/7 to approximately 6,000 residents. Geared towards George Mason students, MCN produces live shows, pre-recorded shows, and student projects. MCN has been providing students with entertainment and news for over 20 years.

Shows

The Pressbox
Sit down and listen as some of the finest talk about what's going on in the world of Mason Sports and Pro sports.

Mason Sports Insider
Tyler Byrum brings you the inside scoop on Mason Sports. He gives you the details, recaps, latest news and upcoming events.

From The Cinema
From the Cinema brings you movie quirky reviews and previews of the movies coming out in the Johnson Center Cinema.

And A Kitchen Sink
Quick, witty, and fiery. Listen close as this short show queues you in on a list of facts that somehow all tie together.

MCNews
Mason's live news program. Airing Wednesday at 5:30 p.m., the MCNews team brings you Mason news, events, weather and interviews,

Upcoming Events

Lemonade Giveaway
April 7th

Faces Of Mason
April 10th

Clock Tower Contest
April 14th

MCN Takeover
April 17th

 /MasonCableNetwork

 MCN231

@MCN231

Mason Cable Network

CHANNEL 231

George Mason University
4400 University Drive,
Fairfax, VA 22030

Email: Mcn@gmu.edu
Phone: 703-993-3996

Building a Backgrounder

PR Writing Stakeholders Want to Read:

How to Pack Your PR Writing Product with Specifics

Writing can be hard work, but it's nearly impossible when you have little to write about. A great way to assist yourself and your clients is to find ways to do research quickly so that you are knowledgeable about the client's organization, products, and goals before you tackle the first version of a writing assignment. The best way to become knowledgeable is to do a backgrounder before you interview or talk with a client, stakeholder, or colleague about your PR writing task.

Backgrounders—What are they?

A backgrounder can be either a formal text you share with journalists and other stakeholders or an in-depth set of notes that only you and your colleagues see but which helps you to conduct effective interviews and pack your work with specifics. That is, sometimes a backgrounder becomes the basis for a fact sheet that you distribute or post. You can see a sample formal information sheet at **http://www.ucar.edu/news/backgrounders/hurricanes.jsp**. Other times backgrounders can also be several-page mini-reports that help you, the public relations writer, to get ready for an interview or a conversation with someone as you write your first version of a blog, release, profile, post, speech, column, or some other public relations writing product.

Getting Started

Find out what your client or your instructor wants to you write. Let's say they want a series of profiles showcasing their top employees. They want to put these profiles on their website. Your job is to interview five or six employees and write a profile on each. Or, you may be writing an in-depth news release about a new product or service. Regardless, you need to do research before you interview and definitely before you write a first version or second version.

Your first step is to find some great examples of the sort of writing you have been assigned. When you get your assignment, respond by saying, "That sounds interesting. I wonder if you have some examples of the sort of writing you want me to do." Seeing two or three examples of the sorts of products you are being asked to produce is incredibly helpful. You can analyze these examples and make a list of what you will need to produce a similar product.

Format

Let's say you are writing an informal backgrounder, one that only you and perhaps your supervisor will see. The format can be informal. Make sure you take these steps:

- Name, date, name of assignment
- Number pages
- Indicate major sections
- When gathering information from the Internet, indicate the source of the information. You are allowed to cut and paste information, photos, diagrams, etc., into a backgrounder used for your personal notes as long as you indicate to yourself that this information comes from a source other than you.
- Length: Probably four or five typed pages.

Gathering Information

The first feature of most good PR writing is that it provides useful or interesting information of value to the client and stakeholders. Let's assume you are doing a backgrounder in preparation for writing a profile of a prominent figure in your client's company. You know you need information about this individual and her accomplishments at the company. Go to the company website and find answers to questions like these. Complete each section.

Questions to Answer in Your Backgrounder

Section 1

Five W's. Is there a key "what" in this release or profile? A who? When? Where? Why? Gather that information. Make sure names are spelled correctly. Titles are correct. Numbers and dates are accurate.

Biography. What are the facts of this person's career? What is her title? What were her previous jobs? How about her education or recently acquired skills? Has she won awards or achieved recognition in other ways?

Confusing terms, structures, or processes. To whom will you be writing? Will they understand the nature of this person's work and accomplishments? Are there a few key terms, structures, or processes that need explaining? For example, an Olympic-level swimmer may be a highly accomplished breast stroker. Will you need to explain to readers what the breast stroke is? If so, what's a good visual or photo that would assist you in this process? Suppose you are profiling a surgeon who specializes in robotically assisted surgery. What sorts of diagrams or photos would you want to gather to help explain how robots assist the surgeon? What concerns might this information raise for readers? What do you want to ask the surgeon when you interview her so that concerns prospective patients have can be addressed? Often you should gather key definitions and explanations of complex structures or processes prior to your interview so that you know what you don't know and can ask your interviewees to help you understand them.

Section 2: History, Future, Geography

A National Public Radio reporter uses these questions to help him learn about topics quickly. Public relations writers can, too.

History. Take this story back. That is, tell the story of this topic, achievement, or individual. What has happened in the past that may be important now in understanding or appreciating the person whom you are profiling? When did the subject of your profile join the organization? How was she viewed initially?

Future. Take this story forward. What is impressive or interesting to you and to others about this person now? What are this person's supervisors and colleagues saying about her? What is surprising, puzzling, confusing?

Geography. Take this story side to side. Who or where are there similar people doing similar work or work that is different in an interesting way? For example, if you were interviewing an Olympic-level swimmer, who are other swimmers that you might compare this individual to? Or assume you were profiling a top business professional in the Washington, D.C., area? Who might enjoy commenting about this person or sharing a story that would help stakeholders understand this person's work ethic and talents?

Section 3

Early first version of your written product. Go back to those writing samples your supervisor or instructor suggested you analyze. Do they have great quotes? Good stories and examples? Good specific facts? The best way to be ready for an interview is to write part of the profile, news release, or blog before the first interview. Let's say you are interviewing a surgeon who does hip-replacement surgery. You know you need a paragraph in your profile about who the surgeon is. You know you need another paragraph and probably a diagram explaining her approach to this surgery, the company she uses for artificial hip parts, and so forth. You can write those paragraphs before the interview and then you will see what you need to clarify or have the surgeon explain during the interview. You will also see where you need a great statement of emotion from the surgeon or a good story or puzzle.

Section 4

The five questions you know you need to ask in the interview. Assume you are interviewing someone very busy. This individual can give you 15 minutes. You want to ask the questions you most want answers to. What are they? Perhaps you need a statement from the surgeon about why she takes pride in her work, or why she believes her approach to hip-replacement surgery is helpful to patients. Or maybe you need a question asking her what her approach is. In short, once you have gathered a lot of information in preparation for your interview, you will be ready to ask good questions. List five of those questions in the backgrounder.

How to Write a Blog

Blogs and the art of blogging are evolving rapidly. Hundreds of millions of blogs can be found on platforms such as Wordpress, Blogger, Tumblr, Medium, Quora, Ghost, and more. On Tumblr alone, the number of blog accounts rose to 226 million in July 2015, up 15 percent from 2011. By August 2015, however, that number had swollen to 250.6 million blogs. The focus and variety of blogs are growing as well, from journalism news to corporate messaging to content marketing as well as personal diary-style blogs.

Q. What makes a good blog?

A. *A good blog is one that people actually read.*

The real question about how to write a blog is to ask why people read blogs in the first place. Think about the last article you read online and ask yourself how you arrived at that site, what you had searched for and why you were searching. In most cases, you were seeking information to help you do something, whether it was how to write a resume or where to find a great tapas eatery. Successful blogs—the ones that people actually *read*— offer *news you can use* or provide value in some practical way. What is *"practical"* is defined by the reader so the first rule in writing a blog is to understand your audience.

Understand your audience: Define the reader by age range, geography, social characteristics (like young urban professional or active but retired baby boomer), and most important, by shared interests (like aspiring PR professional, vegan cooking, triathlete, etc.) As you begin to write, direct your writing to that person and what he might find valuable.

Define your message: The length of blogs varies but whether you choose to write a 250 word or a 1,000-word blog, make every word count. Decide precisely what message—what practical value— you want to convey and don't stray from that central message.

Comm 388 Fall 2015 Course Blog

Provide substance: Use credible, authoritative sources and share or link to relevant material by credible sources. Don't be vague but offer substantive, actionable information. That's the difference between a) Washington Dulles Airport is a busy airport, and b) Washington Dulles Airport ranks as the nation's 22nd busiest with more than 20 million passengers in 2014.

Be pithy, give context, be concise: Don't make your reader muddle through a long introduction of your topic: get to the point quickly. Do provide *context*, like the introductory paragraph (above) to this guide. Studies indicate that people don't read blogs in full but somewhere less than 30 percent of the total content. Edit rigorously to eliminate unnecessary words and phrases and keep your blog concise.

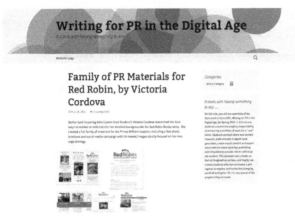

Comm 391 Spring 2015 Course Blog

Use visuals: People absorb visual content more than 60,000 times faster than text. Choose visuals that both attract attention and help you tell your story, but verify licensing of the image and follow instructions for attribution.

Adopt professional standards: Blogs often adopt a style far more informal than the academic writing you master in college. A blog that meets professional standards doesn't have to be stuffy and formal but should be free of errors in spelling, punctuation, and grammar, use fairly short sentences, be unequivocally accurate, and be clear and unambiguous. Conversational style is not only acceptable but is easier to read.

Match the title and conclusion: Wrap up the blog by emphasizing your key takeaway. Did you deliver what you promised in the title?

PR & SOCIAL MEDIA BLOG

DATE POSTED: September 17, 2015
AUTHOR: Sierra Medellin

Starbucks' Fall Formula

It's a perfect fall day: You're wrapped in a cozy sweater to keep out the brisk breeze while crunching underfoot are the fiery shades of fallen leaves. According to many Starbucks consumers, the only thing missing from this idyllic scene is a Pumpkin Spice Latte. Since its launch 11 years ago, the "PSL," as it is referred to by devotees, has become synonymous with the season. Dubbed by Starbucks as the "Official Drink of Fall," its wild popularity is due to their ingenious usage of scarcity and relevancy.

Starbucks has successfully established an extremely effective trigger, a cue that stimulates people to think about a specific idea or product. In his insightful book Contagious, Jonah Berger examines the intricacies of why a particular behavior, item, or notion becomes so popular amongst the masses that it is considered viral. One of the common characteristics of "viralness" he introduces is the proper application of triggers. When there are unique elements of a person's environment that they can easily link

to product or concept that shares a similar thematic nature, they are far more likely to remain aware of it. With this in mind, Starbucks purposefully created a limited, especially autumn inspired drink specifically for the time of year in which most people are looking for something to warm them up. It has become so ingrained in our memory that with the arrival of fall, we anticipate the arrival of the Pumpkin Spice Latte.

therealpsl ● [FOLLOW]

Pumpkin Spice Latte The official Instagram for Fall's official beverage ☕🍂
From: @Starbucks twitter.com/TheRealPSL

23 posts   19.1k followers   51 following

For many the two have become inseparable. The #PSL hysteria is encouraged by Starbucks through multiple social media accounts dedicated solely to drink. This year, the company offered early access passes to randomly selected Twitter followers of @TheRealPSL that allowed them to fill their craving before the September 8th release date. This additional exclusivity heightened the hype surrounding the product and secured its viralness. With the recent change in the weather, the crowds are already lining up.

Writing for Television and Radio

If there is one thing in our lives that is a constant, it is the ubiquity of television shows and radio programs. Every season brings a new slate of shows, star personalities, etc., for us to meet, assess, and ultimately either accept or reject. That, however, is but one aspect of television and radio. The other is the ongoing presence of news and/or talk shows. While these, too, may have ever-changing hosts and/or anchors, they have been and will continue to be part of the broadcast world. These programs and the men and women who drive them are vital sources of information for the general public.

All of us rely heavily on television shows and radio programs for day-to-day information on how we should prepare for the day ("Today there is an 80 percent chance of rain."), what is going on in the world around us ("The nation's unemployment rate dropped to 5.3 percent this past month, according to labor statistics released by the government."), how we might feel about something ("The President's policy toward the Middle East is a mess.")

Because of the role television and radio play in providing information to the general public, they remain key vehicles for those in public relations to try and utilize as ways of reaching elements of society that are of interest to their clients and organizations. An example of this can be found among those working in media relations for George Mason University. Each year, the university's primary governing body, Board of Visitors, considers raising tuition. As a way of helping explain to the general public why it is considering such action, the university's media relations team may decide to use local television and radio outlets to communicate their particular messages.

Following, then, are some general tips on how they might frame their messages to best fit the preferred formats of television and radio (Keep in mind, that most broadcast stories are two to five sentences running anywhere between 10 and 30 seconds. That means all broadcast stories must be concise and with little detail other than the basic facts):

- Use everyday language
- Use ordinary, one- and two-syllable words whenever possible
- Write short sentences
- Use one idea to a sentence
- Use the present tense if possible
- Try to confine stories or articles to one major theme
- Use vigorous verbs
- Use active, not passive verbs

- Begin sentences with a source, use paraphrased quotes
- Avoid starting stories with a dependent clause

Good and Bad Examples

WRONG: Hoping to keep college affordable, George Mason University's Board of Visitors is considering only a slight tuition increase for the coming academic year.

RIGHT: George Mason University's Board of Visitors is considering a slight tuition increase to ensure college remains affordable.

WRONG: George Mason University is going to consider raising tuition for the coming academic year, the Board of Visitors said today.

RIGHT: George Mason University's Board of Visitors says it is considering raising tuition for the coming academic year.

Public Service Announcement Example

George Mason University is sponsoring a 10k run to help support National Cancer Awareness Month. Open to the general public, the event is set for Saturday, October 3, beginning at 8 a.m. Participants are to report to the Patriot Center at the university's Fairfax campus. For more information, call 703-993-xxxx.

Speechwriting

This may seem obvious, but nevertheless it is a truism that must be emphasized and not forgotten by those write or attempt speeches for others: The speech you compose is not about you. You should never think of yourself as some sort of puppet master attempting to use others to let audiences how you feel about various topics. As a writer of speeches, your job is to put yourself in the shoes/mind/heart of the speechmaker. The speech is about presenting the speaker in a positive light, showcasing the topic and helping create a connection between the speaker and the audience. Again: it is not about you. Given this reality, speechwriters are generally folks who prefer being behind the camera, not standing in the spotlight or being the focus of attention of others. This is not to say, however, that speechwriters are not vital players in the overall process of establishing and maintaining strong, positive ties between various publics or entities. Their function is extremely important—just not overtly visible.

Before writing a speech—any speech—there are several basic questions the writer must ask him or herself: (1) Who is giving the speech? (2) Who is the speech for? and (3) What is the purpose of the speech? Without having a strong understanding of the answers to those questions, then any chance a writer might have of writing something that will adequately resonate with the intended public and generate a desire response are greatly reduced. Remember: public relations workers are all about establishing and maintaining strong relationships. Thus, speeches must be written in such a manner as to help the person giving the speech strongly connect with those on the receiving end of their remarks. (Keep in mind: those receivers are not just the folks in the audiences. There are others, often more than you might realize, who will read the speech after it has been given. In the case of the media, it is even possible they may report on what the speechmaker had to say.)

Key Elements (the "Three Knows")

(1) Know your speaker

Does the speaker have a certain way of speaking they prefer or that is unique to them? Remember: the speech you write is about the speaker and helping them connect with their audience. The more you can do to showcase the speaker's personality as a way of helping building a bridge between them and their audience, the greater chance the speech will be one of significance.

(2) Know your audience

What are their concerns? Hopes? Dreams? Who are they? The better able you, the speech writer, can answer these fundamental questions, the better you will be able to make what you write relevant to the audience. This does not mean the speaker has to say what the audience wants to hear. Rather, it means the speaker will be in a more commanding position to say what the audiences to hear about.

(3) Know your topic

The deciding factor in terms of what makes a speech effective is its content. Is there substance to what the speaker says? Do the remarks contain facts and concrete information that can help enlighten members of the audience? To achieve these objectives requires research. As the writer of the speech, you need to become a mini-expert on the topic. Then, in terms of writing, your challenge will be to match this information with what is of interest to the audience. When it comes to speeches, yes, audiences enjoy being entertained. But more than that, they wish to be informed. You the speechwriter can make that happen.

When it comes to speech writing, there are other "knows" as well, of course. These include knowing the venue in which the speaker is going to speak, knowing the amount of time which the speech is being allocated, and knowing the purpose of the speech. Collectively, this information helps provide the speech with specific parameters that, in turn, can help shape its actual content. If the venue, for instance, is a small conference room, then the content can be more intimate and conversational. But if the speech is to be given in a large arena, then what is said can be more flowery. In terms of purpose, is it the speaker's goal to motivate the audience to take certain action ("Go out and vote for me!") or is it to inspire ("Be the best you can be.") Ultimately, it is the speech's purpose that drives the content and how the speech itself is delivered.

Business Speech Template

What is a "business speech?" What are the fundamental ingredients that distinguish it from a testimonial or eulogy? Business speeches represent public remarks in the context of a professional setting, such as a corporate gathering or professional setting. The content revolves around information pertaining exclusively to an entity's standing or advancement. They can touch on personnel issues or even specific individuals as well as such impersonal themes as profits, promotional campaigns, and year-end assessments or reviews.

In terms of the actual format, following is a general outline of how a business speech should be presented, including some of the key points needing to be touched on:

I. Introduction

- Thanking audience for their attendance
- Recognizing key individuals in audience
- Stating purpose of speech; "Today I am going to talk about our company's goals for the coming year."

II. Body of Remarks

- Key points to be made

- Explanation of why these points are important to audience—why they should care

- Relevant historic or background information

- Examples that best illustrate each point

III. Summary/Conclusion

- Review of key points

- Calls to arms. Direction as to what the audience should do about or with this information ("Go out and vote." "Write your Congressman." "Talk with your supervisor.")

- Reiterate appreciation for audience's attention and interest.

Section III

The Public Relations Plan

Advice from the Real World:
Mason Alumni Share Advice

Ariel Brown, Class of 2014
Communication Associate, Reingold, a strategic communications firm, Alexandria, VA.

Initially, I was nervous about committing to public relations as a concentration because it didn't have a clear cut career path—so I took the classes without interning anywhere. I wish I would have taken the leap and just applied for PR internships so I would have had more experience coming out of undergrad. I would tell any PR student to trust your gut and pursue PR if that is what you're passionate about. You won't regret it.

Chapter 6

PR Research and Planning

Advice from the Real World:
Mason Alumni Share Advice

Melanie Moore, Class of 2014
B.A. in Communication, Public Relations
B.A. in Art History
Minor in Tourism and Events Management

Even after choosing to study public relations, I was not 100 percent convinced that it was right for me until I worked at my first internship. No matter what your concentration, I cannot stress enough the value of real world experience. Yes, you need to get good grades and participate in class, but an internship, part time job, or volunteer position makes your high GPA look even better. Think of the internship as a trial run; only after you experience PR for yourself, outside of the classroom, will you truly know if it is right for you.

Make sure you use the resources George Mason University affords you as well, such as being involved in student run organizations like PRSSA or a business fraternity, where you can meet alumni and other professionals who have worked in the field. Over time, I realized that the greatest resource George Mason has is its professors. Many professors are subject matter experts and are able to share valuable, first hand experiences with you about what to expect and how to be the most successful in the future. All you have to do is ask!

Public Relations Planning

Public relations planning is a disciplined process. Following a disciplined approach is what helps make a public relations plan strategic. *Strategic communication programs are research-based and objective driven.* That means the plan is based on knowledge (derived from primary and secondary research) and is created to achieve very specific and measurable objectives.

Step #1: Define the challenge

Your public relations plan has a job to do. Understanding that mission—the problem or challenge to be addressed—takes a serious and deliberate effort. *Due diligence* in public relations mandates that you learn about your challenge and become fully informed. You may not be an expert in the topic area but you must know what all of the experts say.

Public relations is viewed as a process that helps organizations solve problems and the problem needs to be well defined. Consider the examples below:

Poorly defined challenge: Create buzz for MasonCakes.

What's wrong with this? Is "buzz" the real challenge? No, but "buzz" is part of the campaign objectives. Generating awareness and word-of-mouth messaging is indeed one part, but only a part, of the overall challenge facing a new small business. The challenge is much broader than this.

Clearly defined challenge: Introduce MasonCakes and establish the new business as a "favorite tradition" or institution among students, faculty, staff, and alumni.

This challenge describes the long-term goal of the PR campaign to be achieved over time as well as the short-term goal. In addition, this challenge identifies the target audiences with whom relationships need to be developed.

Step #2: Conduct Secondary Research

Secondary research is a misnomer as it is often the *first* step in the planning process. Secondary research, sometimes called desk research, is the gathering of information that already exists. Someone else has already done the work; you are selecting the most relevant information and collecting it. Secondary research is virtually anything you can find that helps you understand your PR challenge.

Consider the source: Don't believe everything you read or hear or see. Seek authoritative, credible sources and be prepared to *attribute* what you learn to these sources. You may need to peel back the layers of an online piece to determine authorship. Be able to distinguish *native advertising* and *brand journalism* (sponsored, paid material) from journalism.

Cite your sources: You should quote and credit your sources or include full citations. Be careful not to present the information as your own. (Only cite your primary research as your own.) Your investigation is enhanced, not diminished, by the number and caliber of your sources.

Objective and subjective material: Seek hard facts, data, and evidence to provide an objective or unbiased look at your challenge. And, seek opinions of stakeholders from all viewpoints. This will help you conduct an accurate *situational analysis*, where you examine the problems and opportunities.

Where to start: Conducting secondary research for a PR challenge is not unlike the research you conduct for your college courses. The library's databases allow you to search large numbers of sources quickly and enable you to narrow your search easily. Google searches provide tremendous results but unless you narrow your search, you may become overwhelmed with the quantity of work to examine.

By the numbers: Collecting numbers or quantities is often a good starting point and helps establish the *scope* of your challenge. This might include

- Numbers of employees or customers
- Dollars spent on a key budget item (paper, fuel, insurance, medicine)
- Number of social media followers
- How many years in business
- Number of offices, stores
- Number of hours spent on a key activity (texting, cooking, commuting)
- Number of items produced in a day, week, month, year
- How many letters received or messages sent
- Number of mass media impressions
- Website traffic
- Ranking in "best" reports

Research, studies, and reports: Look for publicly available research in your challenge topic area. Seek authoritative authors and publishers such as:

- Federal government departments and institutes (like the U.S. Department of Labor, the National Institutes of Health, U.S. Census Bureau)
- State and local government departments (like Virginia Department of

Education, Fairfax County Economic Development Authority, Fairfax City Data)

- Professional associations and journals (like Journal of American Medical Association, National Association of Manufacturers, Automobile Dealers Association, National Petroleum Institute)

- Nonprofit organizations (like Sierra Club, UNICEF, UN Foundation, International Red Cross)

- Public opinion consultants and industry research (like Pew Research, Gallup, Forrester, Fortune 500)

News Media: Traditional, online, and social media reports are critical to your understanding of your PR challenge in *real time*. Your secondary research must include a thorough review of mentions of your client or challenge explicitly or implicitly in everything from the New York Times to the local online news site. Social media platforms offer you the opportunity to *listen* to what others are saying about your challenge.

Step #3: Conduct Primary Research

Market research, a $21 billion dollar industry, is used extensively in business and by public relations firms, ad agencies, and marketing companies for planning, testing, and measuring. The research phase of the traditional four-step model of public relations involves both *primary* and *secondary* research.

Secondary research is collecting and summarizing information of others, like reports and studies, news articles, and scholarly journals.

Primary research is what you can collect on your own, directly from a source, using interviews, surveys, and observation. Primary research will help guide program development because you can get reactions to your ideas, suggestions for approaches, test effectiveness of messages, and gather other feedback *before* committing to a plan of action. Try using primary research tactics for your courses to get a sense of how market research impacts product launches, public information campaigns, and issues management efforts.

Primary research is exploratory and is considered *qualitative* rather than quantitative research when it is:

- Smaller sample size, 30-40 participants or less

- Selection of participants is not random but usually selected based on willingness and availability

- Less structured and less formal inquiry seeking to elicit reflections, opinions, attitudes, and perceptions

- Results are not projectable. Results only reflect the participants' opinions, not the demographic group they might represent.

Quantitative research then is a large enough sample size as to achieve statistical reliability; participants are chosen randomly from the target demographic; inquiry is highly structured, seeking specific information; and the results may be projected (at plus or minus a certain percent) to reflect the majority of the target demographic

Try using *primary* research tactics for your courses to get a sense of how market research impacts product launches, public information campaigns, and issues management efforts, through one of these qualitative methods:

- **Interviews:** One-on-one interviews can be conducted in person, on the phone, by email or online platforms. In-person, telephone, and face-to-face (Facetime, Skype, etc.) interviews offer you the flexibility to easily adapt your questions based on the person's responses and often provide more information; it is easier to talk than type. Chat, texts, and email might be more convenient and less personal or intrusive, which some might prefer.

- **Focus groups:** A focus group is where several people are gathered together for a Q & A and discussion. Participants are usually chosen to represent shared characteristics of the target audience. A moderator leads the discussion through a predetermined list of questions or topics.

- **Surveys:** A simple survey involves a series of questions with yes/no, a scale or multiple-choice answers. The survey may be completed in person but is usually distributed and collected via hard copies or online, through a service like Survey Monkey (**https://www.surveymonkey.com/**).

- **Observation:** Monitoring or observing behavior can be helpful in establishing a pre-campaign benchmark or post-campaign results, as well as offering insights into customer or consumer behavior.

Advancing technologies will continue to make qualitative research easier to conduct through webcam interviewing, online communities, and bulletin boards, even Twitter chats.

Purdue University's OWL Online Writing Lab (**https://owl.english.purdue.edu/owl/**) is a terrific resource for students to begin practicing primary research techniques. Start with "What's Primary Research and How do I Get Started?" (**https://owl.english.purdue.edu/owl/resource/559/01**)

Step #4: Synthesize And Analyze

In many of your assignments, you will be asked to conduct research, synthesize what you have learned, and then analyze it. What does this mean? The ability to *synthesize* and *analyze* is one of the reasons why jobs in public relations are considered highly creative.

The process of synthesizing and analyzing forces an examination from many perspectives and routinely leads to innovative problem solving.

Synthesize: Dictionaries define the verb synthesize as to combine a number of things into a new, coherent whole.

If you are assigned to write a case history of an integrated digital campaign or a communication crisis, you will need to *synthesize*. You will conduct research among a variety of sources: agency websites, industry blogs, scholarly journals, news articles, PRSA case files, and more. From this information, you need to create a document, which might take the form of a professional business memo or a traditional academic paper, which is your *new coherent whole*.

- **Seek a pattern:** To synthesize the information you've obtained, you will need to categorize it into like sections. For example, a results section might include what the agency reported the campaign achieved statistically but it should also include what other industry professionals might have written about the success of the campaign.

- **Be selective:** Do not include everything even though it demonstrates that you conducted thorough research. Include the most significant pieces of information or most important, as well as that which comes from the most authoritative sources.

- **Avoid redundancy:** Your research will usually unearth duplicate material. You may find five articles that all report statistics on number of tweets per minute or website traffic growth or an increase in public awareness. Summarize these reports into one succinct section.

- **Use inverted pyramid approach:** In each section, be sure to provide the most compelling information first and the rest in descending order of importance.

Analyze: To analyze is to examine something methodically and, in business, it is often the opposite of synthesize. When you synthesize, you are pulling what might be disparate parts or pieces of information together. When you analyze, you are now breaking the whole into component parts to consider cause and effect, to compare and contrast, to consider what might be missing or could have been improved. Your analysis is your evaluation of your synthesis. For an analysis of a campaign case history, for example, prompt yourself with these questions:

- How is this similar to other campaigns?
- How is this different from other campaigns?
- What tactics seemed to be the most effective? The least?
- What role did timing play in the success of this campaign?
- How much impact did the budget have on the results?

- Did this strategy seem appropriate for the target audience?
- Would this campaign succeeded in a different geographic region?
- Would traditional media been as effective as social media?
- Do the results indicate real engagement or limited participation?
- Was the objective too narrow? Or too broad?

Step #5: Situational Analysis

You've done your homework—you've completed secondary research review, conducted primary research and you have synthesized and analyzed what you have learned. What does this all mean?

Before you tackle writing your PR plan outline, you need to commit to what you see as the problems and opportunities facing your PR challenge. Business often refers to this as **SWOT**, an examination of *strengths, weaknesses, opportunities,* and *threats.* The semantics don't matter as much as how clearly you describe your *situational analysis.* A clearly defined analysis will help you to define the next steps: objective, strategy, and tactics. Keep your analysis simple, clear, and concise.

Problems: First identify the problems, which would include weaknesses or threats. *Problems* are issues your PR plan must confront, avoid, anticipate or try to obviate or overcome. To identify problems, look to your research and ask:

- What stands in the way of a successful campaign?
- What lies ahead (planned events, legislation, programs) which might negatively impact our efforts?
- Where is our organization weakest? What are our negatives?
- Where does our competition beat us?
- What characteristics of (our organization/product/issue) are perceived negatively?
- What aspects of (our organization) receive unfavorable social conversation?
- Who or what opposes this effort?

Opportunities: Now look at what your challenge or organization has going for it; what are its positives, its benefits, the traits or actions that work in your favor, that will help you succeed. An *opportunity* is a favorable factor in the overall environment, like a trend or a change or an overlooked need that increases the relevance or effectiveness of the project in question. You can seek to "exploit" the perceived opportunity through your messaging to key stakeholders. Look to your research and ask:

- What are our advantages in this situation?
- What are the factors on our side, things that will help us?
- What do we do better than others?
- What do people like about us?
- Why do people want/care about our product/issue?
- What lies ahead (planned events, legislation, programs) which might positively impact our efforts?

Completing this process will help you to decide the specific measurable **objective** for the PR plan and the strategies you'll employ to try to reach it. The process is not difficult but takes discipline. Consider how you might apply this process to something about which you are very familiar. Based strictly on what you know, what do you see are the problems and opportunities?

Sample PR Challenge: Improve the environment for hot dog sales. (All brands; a generic campaign.)

Problems	Opportunities
• 'Bad for you' reputation	• Inexpensive
• Suspicious ingredients	• Tasty
• Fattening	• Feed large group at low cost
• High in calories	• Hand-held, no plates needed
• High in fat	• Convenient, easy to cook & serve
• Present choking problems for kids	• Pre-cooked, just heat through
• Toppings make them messy	• Linked to baseball "national pastime"
• Need to supply condiments	• Reminds of childhood
	• Fun, cookouts, neighbors, family

Discipline the PR plan to address these problems and take advantage of the opportunities.

Next Step: Writing the PR Plan

Planning Worksheet

Writing for Public Relations

Getting Started
Planning Worksheet

1. Client Basics • Formal or legal name of client • Address, website, phone numbers • Primary client contact name/info • Other "basic" info: subsidiaries, retail hours, days of operation	
2. What and Why • What does this organization do? • Identify in simple terms the WHAT and the WHY of this organization.	
3. Public/audiences • Identify the INTERNAL and EXTERNAL publics. • An association or nonprofit may have internal audiences that are employees as well as members. • A corporation will have several external publics, including their customers or users as well as other businesses an investors. • Which are the PRIMARY target audiences?	
4. Client by the numbers: get the stats • Outline all relevant numbers you can think of: how many employees, how many customers, members or users. • How long in business, how far do they reach, annual sales, annual volume, most popular event/product, daily/weekly/ monthly traffic or uses, how many Facebook friends, Likes, tweets, etc.	

5. Competitive Environment • Identify other organizations that are direct competitors to your client. Bigger, better, newer? • Identify organizations that are similar to your client. How does your client compare? • Advantages and disadvantages or positives and negatives?	
6. Context • Examine the environment within which your client operates, such as hospitality, philanthropy, online retail, brick and mortar retail, services, etc. • What issues are impacting this arena? • Do you see certain trends in how business is conducted? • What issues might impact your client directly?	
7. Past, present, and future • What is the story of your client? How did it start and develop? What is its current status—quantitatively and qualitatively? • What are future prospects and plans? • What goals? Specific objectives?	
8. Humanize and Values • Who leads (or founded) this organization and what is his story? Is there some one or some thing particularly interesting? • Is this organization involved in community activities? • Do you see it as socially responsible? How? Does this organization "give back?" • Do their publics have trust in this organization?	

9. Media audit/media relations • What media have covered or could cover your client? • What and how are they mentioned in news media? Do they have a media relations activity? If so, how is it conducted—ad hoc or planned? • What media coverage would be most beneficial? Which media?	
10. Communication audit • How is your client currently communicating with various audiences and the media? • Examine the website, brochures, sales materials, outreach: are they professionally produced? Do they convey the brand effectively? Are pieces missing? Are all publics served by these materials? • Are certain avenues/platforms/outlets untapped? • What, if any, would your client like to see you produce? • What are the objectives for the written materials? • Does your client have a strategic message?	
11. Analysis • What problems do you see? Can you identify a way to address those issues? How could your work address these problems? • What specific opportunities do you see? Do you see a way to take advantage of these opportunities? What could you do/produce to address these opportunities? • What are your strategic recommendations for your client? What will you produce and for what purpose and audience?	

Chapter 7

Writing the Plan

Advice from the Real World:
Mason Alumni Share Advice

Hussain Al-Mutawakil, Class of 2015
Public Relations Manager, Sahouri Insurance & Financial

"Press releases. . . own them in class before they own you in corporate America."

When Hussain returned to campus in fall 2015 to share his advice with students in Professor Mims' Intro/Principles of PR course, he made an impression. In their mid-term test, students wrote about his talk:

- I took away that it is okay to struggle. However you can overcome those struggles by being confident in your skills. . .

- Hussain stressed the importance of self confidence. . . we should never compare ourselves to someone else

- He said you needed to create your own opportunities

- He opened doors for himself

- Don't be afraid to be yourself

- Don't be afraid to put your ideas out there

- Be passionate, punctual, and confident

Introduction to GOST:
Goals, Objectives, Strategies, Tactics

The five steps outlined on the previous chapter are the most time consuming and, in many ways, the most difficult part of creating a PR plan. That preparation, however, leads you to what many in the business would say is the most stimulating and truly fun aspect of working in public relations.

- What do we propose to do?
- What problem will we attack?
- How will we motivate the behavior we seek?
- How can we make people care?
- What is our message?
- How can we generate media and public attention?
- What do we need to do to break through the clutter?

Using the GOST template: Presented here is an outline for you to follow in drafting a PR plan or proposal. It is by no means the only way to craft a plan. A PR plan to introduce a new product, like a new app, will be very different from one to develop public support for a new local water conservation program. How your final plan is organized may need to vary from the sample PR plan presented here, however, the basic elements of the plan (**G**oals-**O**bjectives-**S**trategies-**T**actics) must be included.

It's a team effort: In 2013, Yahoo's new CEO Marissa Meyer abolished its work-at-home policy and ordered everyone back to the office. Why? Face-to-face interaction was necessary, she directed, to foster a greater collaborative culture among employees. Other companies moved toward similar policy changes for the same reason.

Collaborating on a plan means that you brainstorm with your team and discuss all possible approaches. Collaboration can turn "good ideas" into great ideas; likewise, those ideas which seemed so great at first, will be discarded as you talk through execution. The old expression, "two heads are better than one," applies.

Goals, Objectives, Strategies, Tactics: The PR Plan

A PR plan is a professional business document. It should be presented on official stationery in a consistent font, with easy-to-follow subheadings. Use of bulleted lists is often a quick-read way to present a series of ideas and actually helps the reader absorb the material.

Look at the Sample PR Plan Outline. Although it is abbreviated (not fully fleshed out) and for a fictitious campus bakery, it is an outline you should follow in developing draft plans for your PR courses. It can be easily modified to match the specific requirements of your assignments.

Introduction: This section "sets the scene" for the reader. In a concise way, present who or what the client or organization is and the "challenge." This is also an appropriate place to summarize (very briefly) what you propose to do and confidently express why you believe it will be effective.

Situational Analysis: This is the foundation for your plan, your "argument" for why you've designed the plan the way you have. The research you've conducted is the basis for your recommendations. Summarize your primary and secondary research; present your problems and opportunities or SWOT research.

Goals and Objectives

What is the long-term goal? PR campaigns are often multi-year efforts designed to achieve outcomes *over time*. Consider the long-term goal of these health campaigns:

- The **Heart Truth** campaign was launched in 2002 to reduce death from heart disease among women and continues working toward that goal today.

- The **Best Bones Forever!** campaign was created to impact the adult bone health (prevent osteoporosis) of girls now aged 9–14

- The **LymePowerOfUs** campaign's goal is to ultimately end the Lyme disease epidemic.

- The goal of Fairfax County's **Community Immunity** is to reduce the incidence and spread of the flu virus and positively impact the overall health of County residents.

Identify measurable objectives: Long-term goals are often ambitious, as those in the health campaigns above. A PR plan tackles goals through a series of specific, measurable and often more short-term objectives. The key word is *measurable*.

For example, consider these specific, measurable objectives of the LymePowerOfUs campaign:

- Build awareness of Lyme disease and the dangers in not getting properly diagnosed and treated.

- Educate and train physicians worldwide in the appropriate diagnosis and treatment of tick-born diseases.

- Give back by raising funds for Lyme Tap, a program which provides assistance for Lyme tests to patients who are in financial need.

Creating Strategy

Understanding strategy can be a bit tricky but is an extremely important concept to you as a student pursuing a PR pathway. Successful strategies have earned PR a well-deserved reputation as one of the most creative jobs. US News proclaimed public relations specialist as the "best creative job" in its annual Best Jobs Rankings.

Great strategies often lead to highly creative and successful tactics. The right strategies have resulted in campaigns that have successfully launched programs and products, enacted legislation, elected presidents, altered the course of history and, simply, saved lives.

A **strategy** is the guiding concept to a campaign—how you will *motivate* the behavior or action you seek; what messages will resonate or *engage* or impact attitude or opinion. Look at the strategy chosen in these advertising campaigns, for example:

- **Bounty's "The quicker, picker upper":** The strategy is to promote the product's absorbency and that it is more absorbent than the competition. Greater absorbency can be a time-saver to the user.

- **Old Spice's "Smell like a man, man":** The strategy is to target the product to women/wives/girlfriends—not the male consumer/user—because women make purchasing decisions for hygiene products in most households.

- **Starbucks' pumpkin spice latte:** The strategy is to create urgency and demand by offering this latte for a limited time only, and to use fall and Halloween as triggers.

- **Geico's "15 minutes":** The strategy is to equate 15 minutes to 15 percent savings; to switch to Geico can be done quickly and save you money.

Is strategy in PR more difficult to create and execute? PR strategies are not more difficult to craft but are sometimes less obvious.

Consider the strategies used in these award-winning public relations campaigns:

- **Movember Foundation's "Movember":** The strategy is to make participation public; participants who grow mustaches become "walking, talking billboards" for men's health.

- **Always' "#likeagirl":** The strategy is to redefine the phrase "like a girl" from weakness and inferiority to amazing and powerful.

- **UN Foundation's "#GivingTuesday":** The strategy is to inject charitable giving into the Black Friday and Cyber Monday shopping frenzy by establishing a specific day for charitable giving.

- **The Heart Truth's "The Red Dress":** The strategy is to use a red dress as a symbol for the long-running, successful campaign messages to raise awareness of heart disease as the number one killer of women.

- **Dove's "Real Beauty Sketches":** The primary strategy for this integrated digital campaign (using paid, earned, shared, and owned media) was to create a video message that the target audience would be motivated to share. The video elicits a strong emotional response (positive, uplifting) of women learning how others see them versus how they see themselves.

In your courses, you may be assigned to develop strategies for dealing with problems, behaviors, emergencies/crises, products or programs. For those assignments, discipline your brainstorming to the message. Postpone discussion about ideas for tactics, what you will actually do. The tactics must be structured to implement your strategy.

Matching Tactics to Strategy

Once the *strategy* is determined, the next intensely creative step is to develop a range of *tactics* to execute the strategy. The tactics are the specific actions in the campaign, the things you do to implement the strategy.

Look at the sample **PR Plan Outline** for the fictitious MasonCakes bakery. Consider how the tactics implement the strategies:

- **Strategy:** Position the product as the perfect self-reward

- **Tactic:** Create and launch "That Exam Takes the Cake" promotion.

  - Leverage exam week as the opportunity to use MasonCakes for self-reward.

  - Invite students to vote for the course exam that "takes the cake" to win celebratory cupcakes for the class.

  - Invite professors to nominate the course/section that most deserves a reward following the exam.

- **Strategy:** Position the product as THE classic, iconic Mason gift

- **Tactic:** Create an ongoing two-pronged MasonCakes Happy Birthday program.

- Parents and alumni—leverage orientations and move-in days to promote a scheduled delivery to children for their birthdays on campus during the academic calendar.

- Create a Birthday Registry program with established groups like sports teams and Greek community. Cupcakes would be delivered on the birthday "From Your Team" as scheduled through the registry.

Brainstorming Tactics

It's been said that imitation is the greatest form of flattery. In public relations, great strategies and tactical executions have been imitated, copied, and adapted. After primary and secondary research has been completed, there is nothing wrong with mining through award-winning campaigns for ideas. Ideas spark ideas, promote exploration and development, and that is how great campaigns are born.

The award winning **Best Job in the World** campaign by Tourism Queensland has inspired similar approaches by many other organizations. In the 2009 campaign to promote the Great Barrier Reef as a destination, people were invited to apply for the job as caretaker of the island and housesit for six months. The job paid a nice salary and included free lodging and island-hopping transit. Applicants were required to submit a video on the public website outlining qualifications.

The campaign resulted in enormous publicity for Queensland and the Reef. Over 35,000 applications poured in from over 200 countries and generated an estimated $200 million in media exposure. It cost about $1 million.

That campaign helped to inspire Mason alumnus Mark Osmun who created "A Really Goode Job" for the Murphy-Goode Winery, which became the most recognized brand-awareness campaign in wine industry history (see **http://www.winebusiness. com/news/?go=getArticle&dataid=74940**). The campaign put the winery in search of a wine lover and social media expert to live the "wine country lifestyle" and share his story over various platforms.

The campaign resulted in an increase in name recognition for the winery through 833 million earned media impressions in just four months, the equivalent of $19 million in ad dollars. More important for long-term growth, the campaign connected the winery to the millennial-generation demographic. Another measure of success? Sales of Murphy-Goode wines rose 74 percent and the campaign won the Silver Anvil Award from the Public Relations Society of America. Of the 2010 campaign, Osmun says:

"I think that the best original—and for that matter, derivative—ideas come from a single person, who in the middle of the night wakes up with the Vision. In the case of the Murphy-Goode campaign, I read an article in the morning paper about the Queensland program, walked straight into the chief's office and said, 'This is a great idea. No one else is

doing it. We should.' That is not always the case of course. For original brainstorming, I prefer including just one or two other people—that way the process is more focused, and the politics and time-wasting that comes from people who lack creative talent is eliminated."

When it comes to original ideas, Osmun says he is from the Don Draper-Mad Men School. "Don Draper says, 'Just think about it deeply, then forget it...then an idea will jump up in your face.' That really happens—all the time," Osmun said. "Sleep on it and let the elves do their work."

Mining Award Winners for Ideas

Awards competition abound. Here are just a few of the largest and prestigious in the fields of public relations, advertising, and marketing:

- Silver Anvil for achievements in public relations (**http://www.prsa.org/Awards/Silveranvil**)
- Clio Awards for achievements in advertising, sports fashion, music, entertainment, and health (**http://www.clioawards.com**)
- Webby Awards for excellence on the Internet across websites, mobile, social, advertising, and online film and video (**http://www.webbyawards.com**)
- PR Daily Awards in 30 categories including PR on a Shoestring, Infographic, Green Initiative, and Pitch (**http://www.prdaily/com/Main/awards.aspx**)
- PRWeek Awards recognizing corporate, agency, nonprofit, and education work in public relations (**http://www.prweek.com/us/awards**)
- Digital Communication Awards for achievements, professional campaigning, and strategic thinking in online communications (**http://www.digitala-wards.eu**)
- MarCom Awards for individuals and companies involved in concept, writing, and design of print, visual, audio, and web materials and programs (**http://www.marcomawards.com**)
- European Excellence Awards for achievements in PR and communication (**http://www.excellence-awards.eu**)
- Wommy Awards for exceptional word of mouth campaigns (**http://www.womma.com/org.posts/2014/08/wommy-showcase-exceptional-word-of-mouth-campaigns**)
- Content Marketing Awards for best content marketing (**http://www.contentmarketingawards.com**)

Matching Tactics to Strategy
Snapshot: Best Bones Forever!

It is easy to see the discipline of PR planning in the **Best Bones Forever!** campaign, partially outlined below. The Office on Women's Health of the U.S. Department of Health and Human Services launched this campaign in 2009. In 2014, leadership of this highly successful campaign was transferred to the nonprofit American Bone Health who continues the work at **http://www.bestbonesforever.org**.

Problem: *65 percent of girls aged 9-14 do not receive enough calcium*

Goal: *Impact the daily calcium intake of girls aged 9-14 to prevent osteoporosis*

Objectives:

- Increase awareness of bone healthy behaviors among girls aged 9-14
- Increase bone strengthening physical activity and consumption of calcium rich foods
- Generate campaign awareness over 3 years

Strategies

- Package desired behavior change in a way that increases benefits, reduces costs and connects with the target audience
- Make bone-healthy behaviors the most desirable choice, a social norm
- Emphasize fun and friendly in all program materials in order to engage, entertain and empower
- Motivate girls to engage and become brand evangelicals
- Launch as a community based pilot and then roll out
- Test and measure behavior change interventions

Tactics and Results

- Engage a diverse partner network
  - Signed 60 partner agreements
  - Participated in 100 partner events
  - Partners developed BBF campaign products for their audience

- Partners placed PSAs in media materials
- Partners contributed ad and event space
- Partnered with First Lady Michelle Obama

- Engage with our audience online and at fun events
  - Created website as central community for target audience
  - Provided downloadable resources for educators/health providers
  - Created interactive games, quizzes, online events
  - Launched Skelegirls display for events
  - Launched dance concerts
  - Launched Halloween Weekend Jam
  - Held a National Dance Contest

The campaign offers great examples of engaging tactics, which are reviewed in more detail in *Social Marketing Quarterly* published an article about the campaign's partnership strategies (**http://smq.sagepub.com/content/18/1/55.abstract**). *Cases in Public Health Communication & Marketing* also published an article with more details (**http://publichealth.gwu.edu/departments/pch/phcm/casesjournal/volume6/files/CasesV6Osborn5.pdf**).

PR PLAN OUTLINE FOR (Fictitious) MASONCAKES

In 2008-9, small bakeries popped up in major U.S. cities with a focus on a single product: cupcakes. Lines formed around several city blocks in New York's Village where customers paid from $2.50 to $4.75 for a single cupcake. Now a major national trend, cupcake sales are estimated to be in the hundreds of millions annually through an estimated 4,372 retail stores.

MasonCakes is an independent bakery about to open on the GMU campus, in the Johnson Center. It is the brainchild of Brandon Backus and Jessica Darling—two outstanding PPR students. The vendor will feature 35 varieties of cakes, including some unique flavors and decorating designs. The cost for cakes will begin at $1.00 up to only $2.50. Delivery is available for orders of a dozen cakes or more.

The Challenge (Goal)

Introduce MasonCakes to the GMU community and establish the new business as a "favorite tradition" or an "institution" among students, faculty, staff, and alumni.

Problems

- Cupcakes are seen as a high calorie product. Mason students, like all millennials, are keenly aware of food calorie content and generally avoid high calorie products.

- Even at $1.00, a cupcake is seen as an expensive, unnecessary purchase.

- Students might prefer to spend a $1.00 or more on competing products, such as specialty coffee drinks.

- Cupcakes are seen as a childish indulgence; our target audience wants to be viewed as adults.

Opportunities

- MasonCakes are a "shiny, new object" and therefore will initially attract interest and attention.

- MasonCakes are unique and different—no two are alike.

- MasonCakes are a low cost treat and much lower than competitive indulgences like coffee or alcoholic beverages.
- MasonCakes will be able to fulfill students' ever-present needs for a "gift" for friends celebrating birthdays and personal achievements.
- MasonCakes are a lower calorie indulgence than coffee drinks or alcoholic beverages.
- MasonCakes remind audiences of childhood celebrations and are a fun treat.

Target Publics

- The target audience is restricted to the GMU population, segmented into students, faculty, and staff.

Objectives (Specific, measurable outcomes)

- Introduce and create measurable awareness of:
    - MasonCakes as a new, independent campus vendor
    - MasonCakes cupcake varieties and price
- Generate, track, and increase traffic to the MasonCakes store.
- Generate, track, and increase traffic to the MasonCakes Website.

Strategic Plan (The "how," motivation, reason, purpose)

- Promote MasonCakes as a "homegrown" business started by "two of our own" to encourage active support of the business by all campus publics, promote loyalty.
- Position the product as a positive alternative to other products for these reasons:
    - Low cost: Latte costs $3.50, a beer costs about $5
    - Lower calorie alternative to coffee drinks and alcoholic beverages
    - These cupcakes are FUN, UNIQUE, CRAZY
- Position the product as classic, iconic PERFECT GIFT to help celebrate friends' birthdays and accomplishments.
- Position the product as THE PERFECT SELF REWARD after that exam, that faculty meeting, etc.

Tactical Plan (The "what," the things you will do)

- Produce a major event to attract all audience and to get attention, break through clutter and stand out. *(In Monroe's motivated sequence, first task is to **get attention**.)*
    - (Include full details on the event, how conducted & promoted)
- Execute a media relations campaign to generate widespread publicity on

campus via every single media outlet. *(Use theory of the two-step flow, agenda setting, opinion leaders, use of social networks.)*

- (Include full details on news releases, interviews, appearances, spokespersons)

- Launch a social media campaign to generate traffic to both the website and to the store. *(Use theory of social diffusion, social currency, game mechanics.)*

  - (Include full details on Facebook, Twitter, Instagram, etc., contests, reward promotions, etc.)

- Create an ongoing two-pronged MasonCakes Happy Birthday program.

  - Parents and alumni—leverage orientations and move-in days to promote a scheduled delivery to children for their birthdays on campus during the academic calendar.

  - Create a Birthday Registry program with established groups like sports teams and Greek community. Cupcakes would be delivered on the birthday "From Your Team" as scheduled through the registry.

- Create and launch "That Exam Takes the Cake" promotion.

  - Leverage exam week as the opportunity to use MasonCakes for self-reward.

  - Invite students to vote for the course exam that "takes the cake" to win celebratory cupcakes for the class.

  - Invite professors to nominate the course/section that most deserves a reward following the exam.

Working Schedule (The "when," think through the execution of tactics)

In this section, create a detailed calendar of work to be accomplished within your key periods of planning, pre-launch, launch, and execution and post campaign assessment. Specific tasks should be assigned to team members with due dates for each item.

- **September 1–30:** Campaign planning, event plans & contracts, production of materials, write and publish media kit and publicity materials, establish social media accounts.

- **October 1–31:** Pre-launch. Establish relationships with influencer groups and opinion leaders; conduct traditional and media relations campaign; conduct outreach to target audience segments; conduct social media engagement.

- **November 1–Thanksgiving:** Campaign launch, major event. Execute plans for the major event and the That Exam Takes the Cake promotion.

- **December 1–15:** Gather and assess results. Prepare final report and oral presentation.

- **Conclude launch campaign December 1** (detail: a calendar or timeline or due dates for specific steps. Should include any items that need to be "produced" like news release, email drop, event promotion, etc.)

Evaluation and Measurement

- Assign 2 team members to count and estimate crowd at kick off event
- Assign 1 team member to count and track website traffic and social media hits (likes, etc.)
- Require store clerks to maintain in-store traffic numbers for two weeks
- Require client to provide daily sales tracking.
- Obtain qualitative measurements, testimonials, product ratings, online rating sites
- Monitor and maintain digital file of all media interviews, articles and mentions
- Monitor and track registrants for birthday cake program
- Quantify participation in That Exam Takes the Cake promotion

PR Plan Outline: Student Example

WeArePR
Principles of Public Relations
Careers start here.

Danna Chavez Calvi
COMM 330-002

PR PLAN OUTLINE FOR THE ALTERNATIVE HOUSE
"Look Good, Feel Good" Campaign

Whether all who have experienced prom truly classify their memory of it as a "night to remember" and a symbolic epitome of their high school years or not, most would agree that having the choice to attend such social events during adolescence should be an opportunity all have. An opportunity and choice that should have little, if anything, to do with being able to prepare properly and afford such. Nevertheless, today the youth, including that of Fairfax County, indeed still struggle with that.

Despite being considered one of the wealthiest and most educated counties in the nation, Fairfax County still faces a constant challenge with the homeless and at-risk youth. Though the numbers have decreased since 2008, not many are aware that the number of homeless families with youth under 18 is still higher than homeless individuals in the area.

The Alternative House is a local non-profit organization and local shelter located in Vienna, Virginia. It was originally founded in 1972 as an emergency shelter for runaway teens, and is currently the only emergency shelter in Northern Virginia. Today, it has expanded to help families, young mothers, and at-risk youth through a range of community-based services, young mother programs, and homeless youth initiatives.

The Challenge

Create a successful donation drive focused on acquiring items for formal occasions to be donated to the Alternative House. The total amount of items collected will be a tool used to reflect an increase in awareness of the organization by the George Mason population.

Problems

- Fairfax County is considered by many to be a prominent affluent county; as a result there's difficulty believing there is a considerable amount of at-risk youth & homelessness

- The Alternative House is not within the grounds of George Mason University (GMU)

- Since a considerable amount of students live on campus, not all students have immediate access to dress attire they no longer need (e.g. former prom dresses)

- If focus is solely on clothes (e.g. formal dresses), it may restrict the amount of items acquired and isolate demographic populations (e.g. the male population)

- Other PPR groups already are seeking donations (e.g. party supplies & old shoes)

Opportunities

- Though not on campus, the Alternative House is at fair distance from GMU Fairfax campus (15-20min)

- The non-profit organization, has a history of over 40 years increasing its credibility and impact on the community

- It has been acknowledged and supported by public figures such as Congressman Gerry Connolly

- Voted 4 out of 4 stars by Charity Navigator, an independent nonprofit evaluation organization, for four consecutive years

- The variety of programs offered at the Alternative House, which have expanded throughout the years to support homeless and at-risk youth, renders an opportunity for clear examples to exhibit the personal impact it has on our local community

- It holds open-door information sessions every 2nd Tuesday of the month to educate general public along with volunteers about the organization's mission and function. Includes tours of shelter and center. This can further entice students to see what the organization is all about with no strings attached.

- Since its mission is a charitable one, it allows the opportunity to partner with student organizations who often have a goal to be of service to the local community. Key organizations may include: Mason U, Scholar for Scholars, and the Social Work Student Association

- The donation drive being centered around idea of prom could provide an opportunity for more effective outreach, notoriety, and sympathy from the public (prom season is April- early May)

- April is considered to be National Child Abuse Awareness Month & Sexual Assault Awareness Month. Since the Alternative House caters to homeless and at-risk youth, whom are often times there due to abuse at home, running behind those causes could also encourage public involvement/donations.

Target Publics

The target audience would be the current GMU population which includes students, staff, and faculty.

Objectives

- ❧ Increase awareness of the homeless & at-risk youth in Fairfax County
- ❧ Increase awareness of the existence of the Alternative House
- ❧ Acquire a minimum of 100 items for donation to the Alternative House

Strategic Plan

- ❧ Generate awareness of homeless youth in Fairfax County & the existence of the Alternative House using a variety of platforms
- ❧ Position the Alternative House as the prime non-profit organization and shelter of impact for the local Fairfax County Youth
- ❧ Entice public to donate via avoiding limitations and creating a competitive friendly partnership environment
- ❧ Seek opportunities to reward those who donate

Tactical Plan

- ❧ "I'm Homeless/At-Risk & You May Not Even Know It"
  - Distribute a bountiful amount of small (index card size) cards/flyers to students solely dedicated to:
    - » Telling a compelling success story of a particular teen who was helped by a particular program
    - » A current teen who believes a particular program is making a difference on his/her life
  - Make sure to card includes the Alternative House logo, its address, AND the fact it is:

    ### The only emergency shelter for teens in Northern VA

  - Make sure to include at the bottom:

    ### *"Want to help make a difference?*
    ### *Help give them a Night to Remember.*

    ### *Donate.#LookGoodFeelGood OR #MASONCares"*

    (Very basic info on what/where/when to donate)

  - These cards should be centered around testimonials/stories
- ❧ Traveling "Informational Kiosk" Day(s)
  - Learn when particular organizations of interest (e.g. Social Workers)

will have their weekly/monthly meeting

- Have one or two team members attend that meeting in order to formally pitch the Alternative House & donation drive to that particular audience

- Representative (s) should be sure to distribute the cards previously handed out to most students, ALONG WITH standard size paper flyers/brochures which include more detailed information:
  » Basic information on the Alternative House (location, mission, programs)
  » Include statistics (e.g. how many teens it has helped)
  » Include poignant/compelling images
  » Accentuate the fact it's the ONLY emergency shelter for teens in Northern VA

- If "You Donate, They Donate" tactic (details below) is adopted, team members must be sure to emphasize that as well during pitch

- Formal Announcement Postings
  - Post flyers on bulletin boards around campus
  - Run advertisement slides on MasonTVs which include basic information of the organization but primarily include compelling imagery
  - All material should include dates on which the drive will take place, where to leave donations, & logo on it

- Expand options, avoid limitations
  - Give public different options of what they can donate
    » Option 1: Formal dresses
    » Option 2: Hygienic products (e.g. shampoo, conditioner, toothpaste...etc.)

- "You Donate, They Donate"
  - Partner with a particular location store such as a local Safeway or CVS, reach an agreement that if X number of items are acquired by Y date, then they will match or donate Z number of items as well to the cause
  - Promote that on flyers, via word of mouth/Facebook, & in Kiosk pitch

- "Look Good, Feel Good" & the Alternative House Thank You
  - Give students a "thank you" item to take away: pin/sticker/pen when they have donated
  - Encourage them to leave an e-mail address so that they may receive a thank you message from someone (hopefully a teen) at the Alternative House

Working Schedule

3/24: Conduct focus groups and surveys in JC about the Alternative House

Look for interested 3rd party local store willing to match X number of donation of items

Reach out to clubs of interest to find out about their meeting dates & possibility of attending those meetings

Note: Informational kiosk dates will have to vary (between 3/30-4/24) depending on response dates

3/26: Begin drafting cards, flyers, & slides to be distributed and displayed on MasonTV

3/29: Group Meeting

Finalize decisions on partner stores, official cards/flyers, and slides to be distributed

3/30: Begin distributing cards to all around campus

Submit any "request for approval" for slides to run on MasonTV & particular flyers to be posted on bulletin boards

4/06–4/24: Collection of items & continued publicity of the Alternative House

4/25: Collection of donated items from 3rd party

4/28: Conduct post campaign survey & count number of items collected

4/30: Analyze data acquired through survey & donated items

5/03: Finalize materials for presentation

5/07: Presentation of project

Evaluation Measurement

- Assign 3 team members to conduct the pre & post campaign survey of 60 students, will measure their awareness of the alternative house & homeless youth in the area

- Assign 3 team members to keep track of donated items and make all aware if turn-out seems to be running low so that all team members may reevaluate the outreach tactics

Section IV

Working with Clients

Advice from the Real World:
Mason Alumni Share Advice

Mark Osmun, Class of 1975
Silver Anvil Award Winner; Mason Communication Alumnus of the Year
winner

The importance of English, of writing, of distilling ideas, organizing them and presenting them in logical, easy-to-understand prose, is the key to all persuasive communication. I'd recommend that students read papers and watch TV news—but not for the content, instead watch it critically and identify the inherent bias in every outlet. CNN, MSNBC, FOX, NBC, et al, have their biased agendas and present (or omit) their facts accordingly. Those  skills are, after all, what PR people do. The only difference is that they are presenting their stories skewed to the agendas of their clients—and in such a way as to appear newsworthy to their audience: the media.

If I were to be back in school, I would take more courses in business than I did before (actually I took none). Back in the day, I fancied myself as some future artist who needn't sully himself with the mundane stuff of business. I did not realize then that everything is business—art, publishing, journalism. . . you name it. And you'd better be prepared for it.

Chapter 8

Positive Client Relations

Advice from the Real World:
Mason Alumni Share Advice

Logan Rice, Class of 2016
President, Mason PRSSA Chapter, 2015-2016

My leadership positions within George Mason's Public Relations Student Society of America (PRSSA) chapter have provided me invaluable experiences and opportunities. I found PRSSA when I was unsure about everything in my life, like what I wanted to do, where I wanted to be and what skills I possessed. PRSSA introduced me to the public relations industry and gave me a niche, all while discovering my skills and passions. It helped  me break free of my comfort-zones and find value in who I am, and what I want to do with my career and my life. PRSSA has helped me grow scholastically, professionally and personally.

Identifying a Client

What's a "client" and where do I find one?

You may be asked to identify a "client" with whom you will work for part or all of a semester course. Courses including Advanced PR, Writing for PR, PR for Associations/ Nonprofits, and PR & Social media each involve work for a "real client." Sometimes the "client" will be arranged by your professor; in other courses you may need to seek and confirm a working relationship on your own.

Many of you are involved in clubs, sports, and other organizations that could serve as your client. The key is to select an organization for which you can execute a very specific project with measurable results. Past examples have included increasing attendance at GMU's women's basketball games, prompting flu shot participation, increasing membership in a new club, collecting shoes for charity, and increasing the audience for campus media. The key is to effect measurable, positive change for your client, which could include change in awareness, knowledge, attitude, behavior (like use, sales, attendance, etc.)

What makes a "good client?"

Businesses and organizations not affiliated with the university are often eager to be a client and allow the student to "practice" public relations. You will be juggling this work, however, with your other responsibilities so seek a client who

- Is easily accessible
- Will meet with you in person or phone/online
- Will provide the information you'll need to execute your assignment
- Is someone or something about which you already have some basic knowledge
- Is not part of a chain, is independent or is a franchise owner
- Is small enough that they might use or appreciate your work

Where do you find a client?

Think "local." Think "family." Think "friends." Students often find their client by simply speaking with a local business, like the small businesses in Fairfax City that you see on the list below. Others look no further than family. One student created a portfolio for a family accounting business. Another produced materials for a sister starting a singing career. Many students use campus organizations as clients.

Examples of "clients" for PR course projects and assignments:

- 29th Parallel Coffee and Tea
- Ace Photo
- Alpha ID (University Rho)
- Alternative House
- Angler Environmental
- Bernie's Deli
- Bridle Paths
- Café GMU
- Coach My Clip social platform
- Davis Ford Animal Clinic
- Directions for Women
- Fairfax County Community Immunity
- GMU Fashion Society
- GMU PRSSA
- Home Contents Video, LLC
- Jouvence Aveda Salon and Spa
- Katherine K. Hanley Shelter
- King & King Associates Accounting
- Mason Cable
- Mason Relay for Life
- Mason Strides for Hope/St. Jude's
- Mason Swim & Dive Team
- Mason Triathlon Club
- Mercedes Benz of Alexandria
- Mocha Café and Pastry, Arlington
- Nike Better World recycling
- Operation School Bell/Feed a Child
- Pentimento Restaurant, Stony Brook
- Red Robin Restaurant, Manassas
- Sisters Thai Living Room Café
- Soles for Souls
- Stephanie Kristina, R&B singer
- The 25th Project for the Homeless
- University Mall Theaters

Client Communication

You will work with a "real" client in one or more of your PR courses at Mason. Whether the relationship is for a short-term assignment or a semester-long project, the experience will help you practice effective client communication. A good working relationship doesn't just happen but is developed through a series of steps.

Understand the business

In order to write even a single 500-word blog post, you have to understand your client's business and the environment within which he is operating. Execute *due diligence*. Use the Client Planning Sheet to help organize what you need to know. Try to learn more about the client by searching online before you arrange an in-person or phone interview to collect more information. You should also be aware of news, current issues, and trends impacting the industry.

Learn the lingo

To enhance the credibility of your written work, learn and use the terminology of the industry in which your client operates. Common terms in the restaurant business, for example, include sous chef, table d'hote, dine and dash, "86," a la carte, family style service, and early bird specials. In a law firm, terms like plaintiff, motion, deposition, liability, subpoena, and negligence are used daily.

Respect your client's schedule

Your client is thinking about his own business; most likely, your needs will not be a priority. Your client isn't aware of your academic workload nor is he thinking about other demands on your time, like a job, sports or club activities. Accept this and plan accordingly. Try to gain an understanding of what your client's workday is like and when is the best time to contact him.

Expect a slow response

Build plenty of time into your plan for completing your work. It may take days for your client to answer your email questions or respond to other requests. He may not be able to meet with you for several days. Always express precisely what you need from your client and the date by which you hope he will respond. Be prepared to be politely persistent.

Use email unless invited to text

Although you may prefer texting, most businesses still rely on email as a primary form of communication. Your client may or may not use his mobile phone as consistently or frequently as you do. He may not see your email message for hours. Adapt to his habits and preferences.

Maintain a professional tone

When speaking with or writing to your client, use complete sentences, avoid slang, and check your spelling and punctuation. It matters. Your messages are a reflection of you and can add to or detract from your credibility. You should be friendly yet more formal than you would be with your friends.

Avoid "death by email"

Make your correspondence *efficient*. Be clear and precise in your message and ask for a specific response. Try to avoid long email chains; too much can get lost or confused in the back and forth. This will save time for both you and your client. Consider this example:

Inefficient email communication

Hello Ms. Spencer:

Thank you for agreeing to serve as my "client" for my writing course. I need to gather some information from you in order to write my first assignment. I was hoping we could get together sometime next week?

Why?

- *What information do you need to gather?*
  - Knowing this helps your client gauge how much time is needed for the meeting and how to prepare for the session.
- *What is your first assignment?*
  - Knowing this helps your client understand what you are trying to accomplish and what the end product will be.
- *When can you meet?*
  - A vague suggestion for meeting means that this email exchange will need several more messages before time and date can be confirmed. Be specific about when you're available and offer more than one choice.

Efficient email communication:

Hello Ms. Spencer:

Thank you for agreeing to serve as the "client" for my upper level Writing for Public Relations course. My first assignment is to prepare an all-in-one fact sheet. I have reviewed your website but still have questions about your products, pricing, and services. I need to submit my first draft on October 14. I'm hoping you'll be able to meet with meet with me next week. Would Monday October 5 at 11 a.m. at your office work for you? If not, I could also meet on Tuesday, October 6 at 4:45 at your office. Alternatively, I could meet in the morning before class at 8:30 a.m. but I know that is a bit early.

Why?

- Details help both parties.
- You, as the author, have clarified in your own mind what you need.
- You have also looked at your schedule and penciled in possible meeting dates.
- The response to this query might be the only email needed to arrange your meeting. This is efficient.

Working in Teams

*"Alone we can do so little,
together we can do so much."*

Helen Keller

Public relations is an intensely *collaborative* business. Whether you are working in a public information office, a full-service PR agency or with a corporate communication team, you will routinely collaborate with others. Collaboration is defined as *two or more people working together toward a common goal.* In public relations, collaboration contributes to creative problem solving because, as you've often heard, *two heads are better than one.* Why? Because working toward solving a problem with others elicits many approaches and each idea that is suggested often suggests several more.

*"Coming together is a beginning.
Keeping together is progress.
Working together is success."*

Henry Ford

Working in teams in business is, of course, different than group projects in college. However, group projects will help you develop good *collaborative skills*, skills that will help you succeed after college. Approach group projects differently than you approach an independent assignment. In a group project, careful *planning*, *scheduling*, and *communication* will help avoid the problems students often encounter. To manage group work, begin with a plan:

- Break the project into tasks; break tasks into parts and steps
- Assign every task to an individual
- Create a due date for each task
- Be specific about expectations; don't assume others know what you know
- Create agreed-upon schedule of deliverables that shows how each team member contributes to the overall project.
- Establish an open-communication pact; each team member will report on any difficulties, missed deadlines

"Teamwork is the ability to work together toward a common vision. The ability to direct individual accomplishments toward organizational objectives. It is the fuel that allows common people to achieve uncommon results."

Andrew Carnegie

Appreciate the interdependence of your team rather than view yourself as just a member of a group. There is a difference. When you are interdependent as you collaborate, you are able to:

- Work toward a common goal
- Co-create
- Share in your success
- Coordinate knowledge and skills
- Make each other accountable
- Maximize strengths
- Minimize weaknesses
- Delegate responsibilities fairly

Professional Memo Template

WeArePR
Principles of Public Relations
Careers start here.

M e m o   M e m o   M e m o

TO: PR Students
FROM: Professor Mims
SUBJECT: How to Write a Professional Memo
DATE: January 30, 2016

Introduction: Use this template for assignments that require a "professional memo" or a "memo to the professor." A memo is a message that is intended to be brief and succinct. It should present key facts and information in a quick-read format using subheadings and bulleted points. Use brief, tightly packed statements instead of full sentences.

Begin with a one or two sentence introduction that states what the memo is about, just like the paragraph above.

Use subheads: Use subheads to create categories of information, such as:

- Background
- The Marketplace
- Target Audiences
- Message Strategies
- Problems

Use phrases: Then present the important points in phrases, not full sentences, with bullets. This contributes to making this a "quick read" document. Be careful to express your point completely.

Note: A memo is NOT an outline. Your statements must be complete thoughts.

Synthesize: A memo reflects your synthesis of information. Your job is to gather a breadth of information and then synthesize it (summarize) for your audience. Do not include everything you've learned. Do include a list of your sources.

Analyze: Conclude the memo with your analysis. Explain what the information means, its significance, its impact, and how it relates to other issues.

Next Steps/Recommendation/Conclusion: The final category should make a conclusion and, if appropriate, identify a call to action, such as Next Steps or Recommendations.

Advice from the Real World:
Mason Alumni Share Advice

Suzanne Mims

M.A., Communication, 2012
Adjunct Faculty—public relations, social media, writing

My advice is to use your time at Mason to deliberately increase your skills. Make a strategic plan to improve in three key ways:

- Technology is infusing fantastic new tools into the field of public relations. Take that leap: move outside of your comfort zone and try new tools now, while you are still in school. Your portfolio will burst with a cutting-edge appearance.

- Be a thinker: practice synthesizing and analyzing. PR is all about gathering the information needed to solve challenges and then analyzing the best course of action. Employers value analytical skills very highly.

- The single, most valuable investment you can make in your future, however, is to develop strong writing skills. The ability to craft writing that is accurate, precise, clear, and concise will make you stand out in every interview and continue to serve you throughout your career.

CPSIA information can be obtained
at www.ICGtesting.com
Printed in the USA
BVHW092118290321
603655BV00012BA/1355